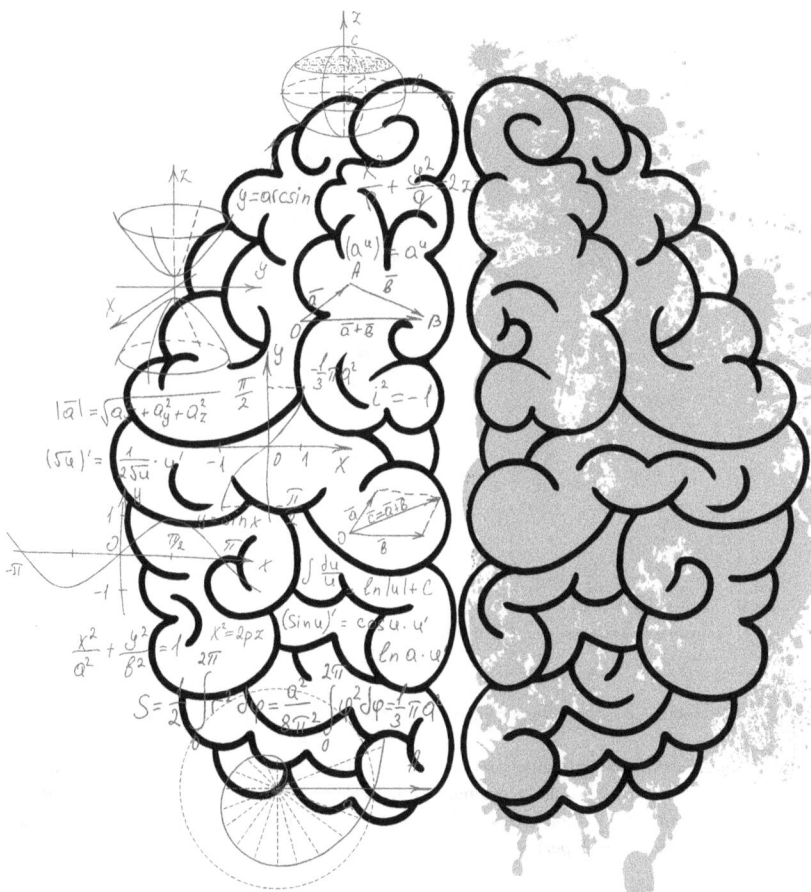

richBRAIN
poorBRAIN

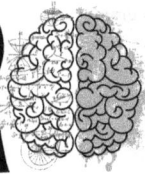

Published by Kejafa Knowledge Works
35 Piet Retief Ave, Monument, Krugersdorp, South Africa
www.kejafa.com

Layout: Christina Harman
Book cover: Jenna Nurnberger, Heystudio
Printed and bound by IngramSpark

First published 2021
First print 2021

ISBN: 978-1-920707-14-9

8-DIMENSION WEALTH

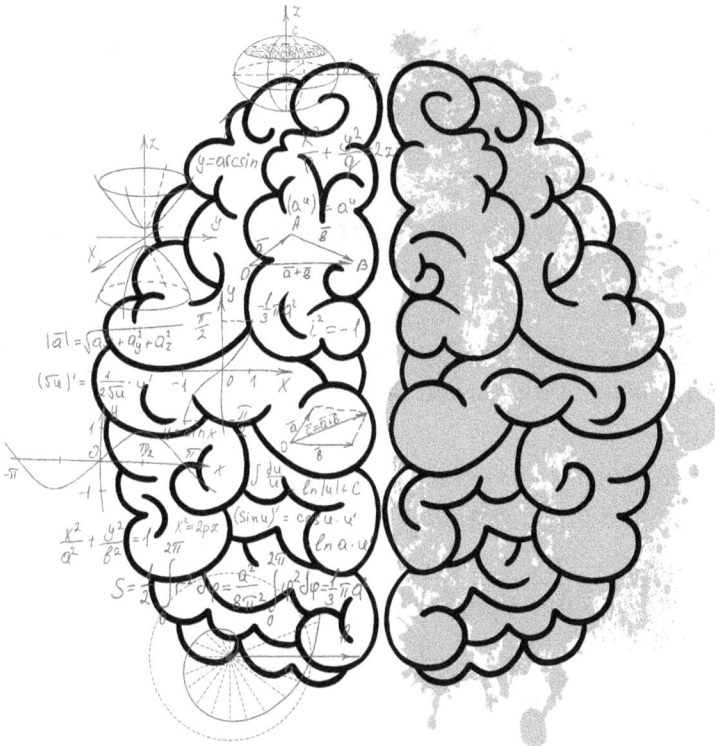

richBR⬤IN
poorBR⬤IN

Dr Kobus Neethling | Wouter Snyman | Dr Raché Rutherford

100-DAY POOR TO RICH BRAIN PROGRAM

The program that will unlock your abundance

- Learn how your brain and your thinking influence your wealth
- Apply your 8-dimension brain to unlock your whole-brain wealth skills set
- Adopt a wealth mindset
- Overcome limiting beliefs
- Get to know how conscious you are about money
- Take ownership of paying your debt
- Create an extra stream of income
- Learn investment basics
- Secure your retirement starting TODAY
- Plan and manage your resources in case of emergencies
- Follow the 29-day Habit changing Diary to establish brain RICH habits

FOLLOW THE LINK:
https://feelgoodmedia.co.za/richbrainpoorbrain

FOREWORD

This book is, in many ways, a continuation of research on applied creativity by the authors. *Am I clever or am I stupid* was an international bestseller, as were *Creativity Uncovered* and *The Ordinary Millionaire*. What became apparent after my seven years of research on the potential of young children was that children in the age range 0–3 demonstrate, what we would call in this book, 'rich brain' qualities.

Often because of 'poor brain' parenting and education, children grow up believing that a rich brain life is just for a selected few. They start negating and disaffirming their natural traits like creativity, passion, courage, and energy and follow common and traditional pathways for which they are most rewarded. They are guided to thinking and making choices that preserve rather than enhance and enrich. We know, and our research has proven time after time, that children and adults of all ages and cultures do not lose their ability to make 'rich brain' choices. These choices can be learned and taught.

In this book, we look at rich and poor brain choices when it comes to our finances. The authors unpack the typical 'poor brain' choices and then illustrate how you can change this disabling habit of choosing 'poor' when you do have the ability to choose 'rich'. The poor brain choices within each dimension of the brain are identified – these are the choices that shape and form our fixed mindset and beliefs. But we all have other rich brain options, and these options are clearly illustrated and unpacked.

Historians will one day go into detail about how 2020 impacted every aspect of our existence. They will also hopefully focus on why specific individuals, groups, and organizations, despite extreme difficulties and crises, thrived and prospered. There will always be tough and challenging times, and if we pursue these with flawed brain thinking and a poor brain attitude, hard times will always overwhelm us. But this book presents the alternative – a rich brain that enables you to thrive financially even in the most challenging times.

The words of Simone de Beauvoir now ring more accurate than ever before:

❝ *Change your life today.*
Don't gamble on the future; act now, without delay. **❞**

– Kobus Neethling

Something to remember

We include a 29-day Life-Changing Diary in the last chapter, Chapter 8. You will be asked to work on one specific goal on your journey to a Rich Brain life. As you read this book, make notes on what you realise you will have to work on, the habits you will have to change, the mindset you will have to develop.

This will assist you in setting a heartfelt goal and launch you on a passionate path of change.

DR KOBUS NEETHLING

D r Kobus Neethling is regarded as one of the leading creativity leaders in the world. He has won most of the prestigious international creativity awards, including the first ever Paul Torrance Lifetime Creativity Award in 2019. He is the author of more than 900 books and 11 TV series (many are international bestsellers) which includes 15 International "Who's Who" publications and he is the Guinness World record holder for writing a book of 110 pages in the fastest time ever (four and a half minutes).

Dr Neethling is the master Whole brain coach of many international sports teams, global corporations, universities, and schools. He is also the Inventor of the world-first 8-dimension brain model used in 60+ countries, translated in more than 20 languages and endorsed by Forbes as one of the top 10 assessment tools in the world. Dr Neethling was invited to train the staff of Nelson Mandela when he became the president of South Africa on the topic: "How to create a culture of creativity".

Dr Kobus Neethling

WOUTER SNYMAN

W outer holds several degrees in finance, including an Honors degree in Investment Management. He is the founder of the attooh! Group of Companies, a boutique financial services group catering for individual and corporate client's financial wellbeing in South Africa. attooh! has won numerous awards and was voted the number 1 Financial Advisory Group within Discovery for the last 8 consecutive years.

Wouter, apart from being an avid entrepreneur, has acted as a keynote speaker, and has been featured in several publications regarding his expert opinion on finance.

Wouter has authored 11 published books, including three international Amazon best sellers: *Would Driving a Porsche Change Your Life?*, *The Ordinary Millionaire* and *7 Simple Principles to Double Your Income*, which he co-authored with Bill Gibson.

Wouter Snyman

DR RACHÉ RUTHERFORD

Raché holds several degrees, including a Master's degree and a PhD on the development of whole brain thinking and creativity.

Raché is co-founder of the Creativity Foundation of South Africa, a member of the Kobus Neethling Institute and has been involved in identifying and developing creative behaviour for over 20 years. She is an expert in whole brain thinking and develops, designs and presents whole brain creativity programs to numerous organisations in South Africa and abroad.

Raché is a keynote speaker and has appeared as a creativity expert on several radio and television programs.

Raché is also the co-author of more than 40 books, including the best sellers which she co-authored with Dr Kobus Neethling: *Creativity Uncovered; Am I clever or am I stupid?; Creative people can perform miracles; Very Smart Parents; Courage; Love, sex and your brain;* and *Do you want to be slim?* **Dr Raché Rutherford**

TABLE OF CONTENTS

Steps to do your NBI profile

1. Request your code from **info@solutionsfinding.com**, to do your brain profile assessment for **FREE.**

2. The link to the assessment is: **https://questions.nbiprofile.com**

3. Fill in your email address and the **code** and **Submit**.

4. Complete the registration fields and remember to **Agree to the Privacy Terms.**

5. Read the instructions and click the box **'I have read the instructions'** and then **'Continue'**.

6. It will then take you to **Question 1.** Make your first 3 choices and then click **'Next question'**.

7. If you cannot complete the questionnaire the first-time round, you have to use the same code and e-mail address when you log in again. The system will take you back to the question following the last one you successfully completed.

For technical support, please contact Marita (marita@solutionsfinding.com) during office hours.

CHAPTER ONE:

BECOMING WEALTHY?

" *Learning is the beginning of wealth. Learning is the beginning of Health. Learning is the beginning of Spirituality. Searching and learning are where the miracle process all begins.* "

How would learning more about my brain and thinking help me become wealthy?

So, a quick question: **"Are you a millionaire?"** Whenever we pose this question, most people respond with a definite "No!" This question has little to do with your wealth status though. It relates mainly to your "mindset" on wealth, i.e., are you living an abundant-minded life versus a poverty-minded one?

Consider the following question for a moment: "Steve Jobs was reportedly **worth $10.2 billion** at the time of his death. How much of this money do you think he would have given away to **spend more time** with his family, loved ones, and business?" We are sure your answer will be the same as ours – Steve Jobs would have given away everything he had to spend more time with his loved ones!

Since you are reading this, in the Steve Jobs analogy, you still have time to spend with family, friends, and loved ones. We are worth billions, not just millions. We just need to recognise that we have so much to be thankful for rather than focus on the things we don't have in our lives if we compare ourselves to the so-called rich and famous.

Further on in the book, we will deal with the concept of your "Rich Brain versus your Poor Brain," otherwise known as your money psychology. This will probably be an essential part of the book for you to grasp since it is a minor focused-on subject with the most significant impact on our financial lives.

In addition to the above, a critical point that you need to understand is that the elusive 'five percent club' who get to experience financial independence **does not** necessarily have a **higher IQ** than the rest of us or grip the proverbial silver spoon in their mouths. Instead, it relates to their taking serious ownership of their financial life on their journey to independence.

You cannot outsource your retirement planning to anyone else but yourself. It is the same as hiring a personal trainer – he or she can guide you to physical wellbeing, but you still need to get up, go to the gym and do the training. If you are lucky, you will have the trainer's guidance for five hours out of a weekly total of 168 hours; then, you will still have to continue your physical wellness journey on your own for the other 163 hours.

Unfortunately, most of the people we deal with spend more time planning their annual holiday than considering their financial wellbeing or preparing for their retirement. We aim to be your planner of choice in your journey to applying your rich brain and achieving financial independence.

Nelson Mandela was right when he said: "Money won't create success, the freedom to make it will."

Understanding your level of money consciousness

We all have a certain level of consciousness when it comes to our lives. One of the immediate levels of ownership around Rich Brain thinking is understanding your consciousness level about your journey towards financial independence.

Let's explain …

Whenever we tackle a new task, we start by being Unconsciously Incompetent – we don't know that we don't know. As a child, most of us would sit in a car and watch our parents drive, holding the perception that it is easy to drive a car. We then move to the Consciously Incompetent level – we know that we don't know. Irrespective of your level of confidence or childlike ignorance, the first time you get behind a steering wheel, it takes about twenty seconds to reach this level. Like most of us, it is probable that your mother hung for dear life on the car door and yelled at you to "Stop"! Once we have reached this second level, we need to put in some serious elbow grease and effort, depending on the level of skill required to advance. We then move to what is known as Consciously Competent – we know that we know. You can now drive around without causing severe bodily harm to innocent bystanders or yourself. However, you still consciously have to go through the motions involved in getting the car from point A to point B.

The last level of consciousness is when a skill becomes second nature – Unconsciously Competent. This level typically occurs after a lot of training and many hours spent behind the steering wheel.

When you reach this level, you may wonder how you got to your destination at point B when you pull in to park.

Answer this quick, relevant question: where are you currently in terms of your level of consciousness concerning your finances and your journey towards financial independence? Are you in that age bracket where you have given up, or do you still believe that you have lots of time left and don't have to worry about it just yet?

Starting your financial independence journey is pretty much like planting a tree. According to an old Chinese proverb, "the best time to plant a tree is twenty years ago, and the second-best time is today." Do not waste one more second – start taking ownership of your journey today! Part of taking ownership is making sure that you learn more about the concept of financial independence.

Being financially independent means precisely that – not being dependent on anyone to pay your accounts. There is no age limit to this, as with retirement. This is merely that point where you can earn a passive income from your businesses, investments, and assets, enabling you to cover your expenses on an ongoing basis. How much you earn has nothing to do with financial independence. We know plenty of professional individuals like doctors and lawyers who make millions annually but are constantly worried about the elusive 'tomorrow'.

When asked what surprised him most about humanity, the Dalai Lama answered: *"Man, because he **sacrifices his health** to make money. Then he sacrifices his money to recuperate his health. And then he is so anxious about the future that he does not enjoy the present, the result being that he does not live in the present or the future; he lives as if he is never going to die and then dies, having never really lived."*

A bank balance that exceeds a million rand **doesn't mean** you are financially independent. Given the current interest rates that you can earn on your bank balance, few people would survive on the return from a million rand.

Consider this: if you invest R1 million at the current return rate, you will generate a monthly income of approximately R6,000 after tax. Could you survive on this? If your monthly expenses are less than R6,000, you would be one of the few who could claim financial independence.

Still, if, like the rest of us, your monthly expenses exceed that amount of return, you would not be financially independent.

So, what is the secret to being truly financially free?

❝ *Money can't buy love, but it improves your bargaining position.* **❞**

— **Christopher Marlowe**

The ultimate secret to being truly financially free lies in not just relying on your active income, being the one where you exchange your time for money, but in using your surplus funds to start generating a second, third, and eventually multiple passive income streams. The aim should be various sources of income, each one being enough for you to live on. In this way, if one source is eliminated, you still have others to fall back on.

Most people that we know who have attained this status make most of their money by practicing a **single skill** within a single industry; in other words, they focus on their core strength and eventually end up developing numerous sources of income around that skillset. Mark Ford, a master wealth-builder, once said about multiple incomes: *"Many Master wealth-builders that we know enjoy a* *dozen sources of income. Some are modest, some amazing. That's the great thing about creating cash flow. Although you never know what will happen with any individual income source, if you get enough of them started, one will turn into a river."*

Understanding the following six simple beliefs around money, will ensure you embrace your Rich Brain almost instantaneously.

1. Only you can take **ownership** of your financial independence – you cannot truly trust anybody but yourself with your money.

2. **It is never** too late to start your journey; however, today is better than tomorrow.

3. All markets rise and fall. **Don't ever believe** anyone who assures you that they can predict the future.

4. If you don't learn to **spend less** than you make, you will never have peace of mind.

5. Most of what you buy when your income is above a million rand is **discretionary**. Do not fool yourself into thinking that you need a bigger house or **the latest model** car.

6. In making financial projections for yourself or a business, always create **three scenarios:** one that shows what things will look like if everything goes as planned; one that shows what will happen if things are mediocre; and one that shows what will happen if things fall apart.

Wikipedia defines financial planning as "the task of determining how a business or individual will afford to achieve strategic goals and objectives." In a layperson's terms, financial planning is nothing but planning and predicting your short-term and long-term financial goals.

Sounds simple, right?

Wrong!

As a society, we have grown so used to living day-to-day and just making ends meet that we have lost sight of the future. But our basic daily financial choices will make or break our future.

Financial planning can be chaotic if you are not aware of the basics. The concept of retirement is changing as we write this book. To rule money and avoid being governed by it, you must learn what distinguishes the rich from the poor. It would be best if you know why you are still running mindlessly in the rat-race.

The simple understanding as to "How you think about money?" will definitely be the first foundation you lay for a bright money future.

CHAPTER TWO:

THE RICH BRAIN MINDSET

" *All money is a matter of belief.* **"**

– Adam Smith

T he Rich Brain Poor Brain book deals with the most significant contributor but most overlooked aspect of wealth creation: your brain and the way you think about money. This chapter deals with your mindset and covers concepts that are rarely discussed yet are some of the biggest drivers towards success and riches. You must pay careful attention.

What should you aim for? How about at least a million?

Why are we using a **million** as an example of a wealth goal? We think people want to become millionaires because one million is a nice round number. It's enough to be life-changing when you have it.

9

Most of us probably know someone who has a million, although they often don't look like it. Many millionaires have ordinary lifestyles. However, many people live millionaire lifestyles – beautiful designer clothes, luxury holidays, costly watches and expensive homes adorned by interior decorators, whose net worth is no better than yours and possibly a lot worse.

What you and other observers cannot see is the cost at which they live these lifestyles: the mounting pile of debts, the heavily mortgaged house, and the stack of maxed-out credit cards. This is not what we mean by a millionaire.

Here we describe the security of R1,000,000 (or more) in cash, investments, or business assets to provide you with an income, perhaps meaning you need never work again unless you decide to improve your lifestyle or your wealth.

We do not include in that million the value of the equity in your home. Although highly valuable, this equity doesn't provide you with the income you need to live on. We are talking about income-generating assets.

Of course, a million **isn't what it used** to be. A millionaire of the 1950s would be the equivalent of a deca-millionaire today, which means having over ten million.

But, let's stick with a million here. If you can accumulate a million, then you'll know how to **keep going** until you have as much as you need or want. A million is a round appealing sum to aim at and to start with.

Does it seem like an impossible dream?

Perhaps you have **dreamed** of becoming rich before, but have done nothing about it because it seems so impossible – too far away even to contemplate. And as you have sat there, frozen, the time has passed you by, maybe years, and you find yourself no nearer to your dream.

It is essential to realise that **every step** you take from now on is another step to your successful future as a financially free person – therefore, not reliant on a job, the economy, or on handouts from the state or your family.

Today, many people have an **entitlement** mentality and assume that it's someone else's job to pay for their lifestyle. Well, maybe it is, but you can only trust yourself to take care of your future and your wellbeing. We will make our own decisions about where we live, what we do with our time, and how we live. This means that we need to have enough money to make these choices and be secure.

There are **many millionaires** in South Africa and the world – and we are not counting those whose houses are now worth a million but who don't have the liquid assets to be secure. There is **no reason** at all why you cannot be a millionaire, too, even if you are starting with less than nothing and you're in debt.

If you have the intelligence and education to read this, you have all that you need to succeed. Yes, okay, you may have more difficulties/commitments/job problems than others. Still, it's time to grow up and stop thinking of excuses. It's time to take action.

> **"** *If you can imagine it, you can achieve it. If you can dream it, you can believe it.* **"**
> — **William Arthur Ward**

Find your why, or you won't last the course.

Becoming wealthy or a millionaire can be a long, hard slog (which is especially true at first), so it is crucial to **know why** you want to be a millionaire (or a multimillionaire). Anyone earning on average more than R2 083 per month will have made around a million rand or more in their working career, yet how many have anything to show for it? (Unless they have been lucky with their home purchase and have increased equity.)

Personally, most of us don't want to own a Porsche or Ferrari, but the thought of it fires up many people. Tell yourself you need to have enough money invested in bringing in sufficient passive income to pay the Porsche's running costs, and there's your "Why".

Maybe you want to be able to **travel extensively** before you are too old to enjoy it. Work out your approximate living and travel costs, how much you need to be invested to pay for these, and there's your "Why." Maybe you want security for your family – there's your "Why".

❝ *Finding my why is the first step in the process. I believe that freedom and being a valuable member of society is my why. Some may find it hard to picture a life that is different from those that they know. Therefore, it is necessary to find a mentor and associates with the same goals. My goal of being financially free includes being able to do what I want when I want and the rewards of a life of my choosing and being a valuable member of society.* **❞**

— Syracuse KT

Reprogram your wealth thermostat

Our subconscious works like a **thermostat**. If it is set to eighteen degrees, the room will have a temperature of around eighteen degrees. The only way to change the temperature in the room is to reprogram the thermostat. Your thermostat is your **mind**. To be rich, you need to **reprogram** your mind for money, success, and fame.

" *If you always do what you always did, you will always get what you always got. You must be willing to do something you have never done before, to get to where you have never been before.* "
— **Albert Einstein**

A 'wealthy' thermostat

" *Wealth, in even the most improbable cases, manages to convey the aspect of intelligence.* "
— **John Kenneth Galbraith.**

Most of us are **wired** to repeat things. We eat the same food, have the same thoughts, drink the same cappuccino, listen to the same music, and carry on with our same usual lives. If your thermostat is set to 'poor', you will always be imperfect; but what if it is set to 'riches'?

Donald Trump, love him or hate him, has been declared bankrupt three times, and yet he is a billionaire once again. He even went as far as to sue a newspaper reporter who dared to call him a millionaire and not a billionaire. You cannot doubt the level of his **wealth thermostat.** His self-belief even moved him to run for the world's ultimate job, that of US president, and attaining it – against most people's views.

Warren Buffet at one time lost so much in Berkshire Hathaway that he mentioned it as possibly one of the worst trades of which he has been part. Today he buys businesses that are in distress. His **thermostat** is set so high that it would simply not allow him to let go of things. Consequently, his mind can find new ways to bring in money, irrespective of the losses he has encountered. Similarly, almost all rich people we meet are **optimistic**. They know that if they lost all their money today, they would earn it back in a couple of years. They know that the most significant difference between the rich and the poor is the amount of money they can hold inside their minds.

Impoverished versus wealth consciousness

What it takes to have a wealth mindset

There are two different types of consciousness: one is **impoverished (poor brain),** and the other is **wealthy (rich brain)**. We all know people on one side or the other, and most people fall somewhere in between, with a mixture of both.

The average South African is living from payday to payday, just trying to **survive**, wanting something better but not knowing exactly what to do or how to get there. Too many people complain about their poor finances and do nothing to change their situation. Just picking up this book is a start; you are now on a new journey – on the road to something better.

There is no doubt that **wealth** is a mindset. To acquire more money, you have to start by changing how you think about money. First, let's talk about how you currently feel about money. The easiest way to discover your beliefs about money is to think about how your parents thought of money. Impoverished and wealth consciousness are taught from generation to generation. It is handed down from parent to child because their parents taught them about money in the way they are teaching you. Irrespective of your past, you can reprogram your future.

Before we continue, let us clarify something about being impoverished and wealthy. Consciousness is a **state of mind.** It is because of this state of mind that people are where they are today. Not just financially, but in other areas of their life as well. This book aims to give you the tools to a **'wealthy mindset'** so that you can have more money in your life, enjoy it, and be abundant in spirit.

To start the process of change, you first need to recognise what you are doing that is getting you the **results** you are receiving. We were not taught much, if anything, about money at school, so many of us might not know the necessary steps to get us where we want to go versus where we are today.

Now, remember, **impoverished consciousness** is a state of mind. It does not matter how much is in your bank account; what matters is how you think about that money. We all know people who are very rich with a few million in the bank. They aren't necessarily the 'flamboyant' type – they're just the rich guy next door who doesn't drive a fancy new car or go out to five-star restaurants every night.

A question to consider: "Do you have a poverty or abundant mindset?" Poverty consciousness or people who plead poverty typically use poverty-conscious words (you may well have used them before):

1. Money doesn't grow on trees.
2. Do you think I am Harry Oppenheimer/Bill Gates or Warren Buffet?
3. Money is the root of all evil.

Or some negative wealth affirmations:
1. I can't afford that.
2. It's too expensive.
3. I can't get that.
4. That will never happen to me.

These are the tools of poverty consciousness, the tools of a poor mindset.

We have all heard of, or know people, who have the money, but they speak these words and reveal their impoverished mindset. Many people believe that the rich are **greedy** people. To broaden the scope, some poor people are greedy, and some middle-class people are greedy. Rich people, who are perceived as greedy ones, have more money. Some rich people are very generous, and some poor people are very generous. On the flip side of this coin, you have to **stop** getting yourself into **a hole** to develop a wealth mindset. And, to get yourself out of a hole, you need to stop digging!

Declare your riches

The start of the journey to wealth is to **stop** doing what you are doing, speaking lack into your life. This is as simple as not saying when something might be out of your price range at the moment or by not talking about the money not being there. Speaking of lack makes it more concrete in your being and more real. Speaking of insufficient money in the bank is just going to get you more insufficient money in the bank.

Joel Osteen, a minister at Lakewood Church in Houston, Texas, tells a story about himself shopping with his friend who kept repeating, "That's too expensive" or "I can't afford that". He then told his friend that by using those words of **lack**, he kept expressing that he would never rise above what he is telling himself and the world around him.

Stop discussing the fact that you don't have enough or aren't able to afford something. When you stop speaking of lack, you stop digging the hole you might be in. If you aren't where you want to be in life with money, you have been speaking lack. This might sound too easy to some, but, as William James – a philosopher and physician of the 1800s – stated, *"The greatest discovery of my generation is that a human being can alter his life by altering his attitudes."*

Co-author Ricki Reynolds, in the book *Endings that Begin*: A Journey into Love, states: *"With the power of our thought, emotion, and action, what we give out comes back to us, first within our being."* She also states: *"Our voice is another powerful sound. It creates vibrations and energy. It carries intent. It can uplift or destroy. It speaks to the universe. God's Word called existence into being. Our voice is a gift God gave to us, and we can use it to create, to manifest into being."*

When you realise the **power** generated within your being when you truly decide, you might start to have a much greater appreciation for your own choices. This will be something that you have to train your brain to do – a work in progress. The importance of decision-making will be realised when you start achieving what you have put your mind to achieve, an essential step towards what you will become or create.

Russ Whitney stated in his book Building Wealth, *"We believe what we say. When we respond to greetings with a mumbled 'I'm doing okay' or 'I can't complain, we build a life that fits that description."*

In his video program *Teach to Be Rich*, Robert Kiyosaki said that the most important thing you have to make yourself rich is **your words.** Poor people use poor words; rich people use rich words. Increase your vocabulary, and increase your wealth.

For example, do you know what 'cash flow' and 'capital gains' are and the difference between them? If you use the right words, you will become wealthier. To learn any subject, you first need to know the terminology and vocabulary related to it.

Robert Kiyosaki makes various perceptive statements that focus on thoughts. These include: *"Our financial problems are caused by the way we think. We have to change the **way we think** about money."* And, *"Once my thoughts and attitude changed, my actions changed, and so did my results."* Finally, *"Leverage can come in many forms. Leverage can be your thoughts. People who win are careful with their thoughts, not saying 'I can't do that. Or 'It's too risky. Or 'I can't afford it. Instead, they say, 'How can I do that?' Or 'How can I reduce my risk?' Or 'How can I afford that?'"*

CHAPTER THREE:

YOUR WEALTH QUESTIONS

G eorge Bernard Shaw states, *"People who say it cannot be done should not interrupt those who are doing it."* A tool for your wealth mindset tool bag is to start, as Robert Kiyosaki suggests, and ask yourself questions such as "How can I afford that?" or "What would I have to do to achieve that or obtain this?"

Asking yourself these kinds of questions opens you up to the solutions. This action links with the maxim "Where there is a will, there is a way". When you hear people say "I can't afford that", what they are actually saying is, "I don't want to put in the effort to try to find a solution to that problem."

Speaking lack is a way out for people. It's a scapegoat. Wealth consciousness includes **looking for opportunities;** impoverished consciousness includes looking for excuses. You were not born a loser; you were born a winner. If you were to ask someone to come over to help you with something you are having trouble with, and that person takes one look at it and says "I can't help you with that", then they are shutting down. The person is not making any effort to try to find solutions to your problem.

However, if that person came over, looked at it, and said, "Well, let's see how we can fix this", and started to brainstorm the different ways that you might go about it, they are opening up other solutions. This is the main thing that the rich do. They look at an issue with money or something they might want and, instead of saying "I can't", they say, "How can I?"

First question: WHAT do you want? In other words, what is your **vision for your life?** Clarity leads to power, and power gives you the ability to do or act. We have seen that the number one reason most people don't get what they want is that they don't know what they want.

So, what do you want? What do you want in each area of your life? The keyword here is "YOU" – what's right for you? Often, we see people living the dreams of their parents or someone else instead of their own.

Question two: WHY do you want this? What is significant about it? This **defines your values.** If most people don't get what they want because they don't know what they want, then the second reason most people don't get what they want is that they don't understand WHY they want it.

Your 'why' is your reason, your 'why' is your motivation, your 'why' is the emotion behind your 'what'. Without feeling, there is no energy to make the changes necessary to achieve what you want. Author Jim Rohn said, "The bigger the WHY, the easier the HOW." In other words, if your reason is important enough, it becomes more transparent and easier to see and develop your plan of action.

Question three: WHY not? Why don't you already have it? What is **preventing you** from having what you want, i.e., what are the obstacles in your way? So, let's say we want something and we don't yet have it. There will be an imaginary reason that your mind makes up to protect you, and then there's going to be the real reason you don't have it.

Uncovering the real reason is critical to get to the heart of what is blocking you. From there, we can make the fundamental changes needed to live the way we "say" we want to live. This question, "Why not?" is even more imperative because, as T. Harv Eker would say, "How you do anything is how you do everything."

Question four: HOW will you get it, i.e., **what is your plan?** What are the methods you will use? It is undeniable that you will need a new strategy or plan to get you there to get from where you are to where you want to be. Our habits are ingrained in us, and without **a new plan,** we will continue to do what we have done in the past, which means we will continue to get what we have gotten in the past.

Without a plan, we will not succeed. The good news is that your plan or strategy does not need to be perfect. It is merely the starting point to a new direction and you will most probably need to make some corrections on the way to your new destination. A Boeing flying from OR Tambo in Johannesburg to Cape Town International will be off course almost 90 percent of the time. The pilot lands safely and on the right landing strip because he constantly makes flight corrections to get his passengers to the correct destination.

Question Five: WHEN do you start and what is the **first action** needed for you to get going? Once we know what we want, why we want it, why we haven't got it yet, and our plan, then we have one thing missing to bring us closer to a result. That is simply to **take action.** Many a great dream or goal has never seen the light of day because it remained just that, a dream! Once you have taken the first action, what are the following steps to ultimately get you to your end destination?

Action is critical if you want to be successful. The biggest problem with most people is that they **think** a lot more than they are prepared to **do**. Thinking is mental; doing is physical. Do you want a dream? Or do you want your dream to materialise? You are only interested in doing one thing at this starting point, one single action step that will get the ball rolling. It is critical because you will set the "Power of Momentum" into motion. As Newton's Law says, *"…a body in motion will tend to remain in motion, and a body at rest will tend to remain at rest"*.

Question Six: How will you KNOW that you are successful? What **measurements and metrics** do you need to determine whether you have achieved your goals?

Success leaves clues! Mark Victor Hansen said the following: *"Big goals get big results, no goals get no results or somebody else's results"*, meaning your results are the critical final step in ensuring you live your dream life. The best metric is to use the ABCs in measuring yourself not just against your ultimate financial goal but against your A or Alignment goal (where do you start), B or Beginning goal (taking the first steps), and C or Completion goal (end destination). Using this simple mechanism will ensure that you have the required metrics in place to measure your achievements.

Your inner world creates your outer world.

One of the biggest lessons that we have learned – and experienced personally – is that two people can sit side by side, using precisely the same **tools and strategies,** and experience a completely different outcome. One person can take these tools and strategies and skyrocket to success while the other person will make no progress at all.

Why would this be?

T. Harv Eker, the best-selling author of *The Millionaire Mind*, said it very succinctly. *"You can have the greatest tools in the world, but if you have just a **tiny leak** in your toolbox, then you have a real problem."* The 'toolbox' in this case is the **mindset** we carry in our heads. It is pointless to talk about success strategies and financial wellness concepts if all the components are not addressed. It is essential to understand that we don't live in just one world. We live in at least four different worlds simultaneously: the **physical, mental, emotional, and spiritual** worlds.

What many people seldom get – and it's something you should clearly understand – is that your physical reality, what happens to you in your life, is nothing more than a **hard-copy** printout of the other three invisible quadrants – the combined results of the other three worlds. In other words, factors such as money/wealth, health/illness, and weight are simply reading the **hard-copy** printout.

We live in a world of cause and effect.

Have you ever heard anybody say that a lack of money is a real problem? A lack of money is never a problem. A lack of money is merely a symptom of what's going on underneath. If we want to change our outer world, we need to start to change our inner world first.

One of the best golfers in the world, Gary Player, famously said *"**The more I practice, the luckier I get.**"* Wealthy people create their own luck.

The 'process of manifestation' has proved to be a valuable concept. It means that your **thoughts** lead to feelings, your feelings lead to actions, and your actions lead to results – it all begins with the way you think. But before we think we all operate from a belief system. A poverty minded person, will inevitably have a poverty belief system.

Belief - Emotion - Thoughts - Feelings - Action - Results

Wealthy people believe they **control** and **create** their lives; poor people think they simply live life. It's like being the driver of a car versus being a passenger. As long as you have a 'passenger' mentality, you will go where other people take you. If you are in charge and 'driving', you determine your final destination.

To be successful start **resetting** your internal mindset, you need to know the building blocks for a successful life.

Considering this statement, what is your current emotional experiencing in life?

Sometimes it is easier for us to describe our emotions than to understand what creates these emotions.

The roots create the fruits.

T. Harv Eker, in his book *The Millionaire Mind*, uses the **analogy of a tree.**

Suppose the tree represents life. Fruits grow on this tree. In life, the fruits are called our results. So, we look at the **fruits** (our results), and we don't like them – there aren't enough of them, they're too small, or they taste sour. In our financial analogy, we don't have enough money (the results of our labour/business).

So, what do we tend to do? Most of us **focus** even more on the fruits (our results) and start worrying more about our lack of money (fruits/results). But what is it that creates the fruits that we don't like? Fruits grow on trees, and trees result from the water and nutrients they consume via their roots. It's what's under the ground that creates what's above the ground. The money we earn and our financial situation has nothing to do with money! They have everything to do **with our roots** regarding money in the way we think about it, how we talk about it, the way we react around money. In other words, our money psychology.

If you want to **change** the fruits, you will have to change the roots. If you're going to change the visible, you will first have to change the invisible. Everything we see that manifests around us is the result of other things happening first. Money is a result, as are health, wealth, and happiness.

Since **lack of money** is the effect, what then is the root cause of our situation? Whatever results we are receiving – whether they are rich or poor, positive or negative, illness or health, always remember they started on a different level. Internally. Our outer world is a reflection of our inner world.

Retrain your brain to release your unconscious power for exponential results

John Assaraf, two-time New York Times bestselling author of *The Answer,* among other books, is the founder of several million-dollar businesses and owner of Neurogym. This company explores **cutting-edge technologies** around a better understanding of the brain. He shares the latest brain-based methods for quickly releasing the hidden unconscious obstacles that prevent people from accelerating their business growth and lifestyle. John shares the same methodology around our lifestyle as we experience it, i.e., we need to

retrain our brains to get different results. His method is based on the simple consideration that our lives result from our thinking, among other factors.

Consider this, **"Why are you in a poor financial state?"** Is it because of the money you earn? Or what you do with the money you earn? Or perhaps you are not making enough money. This leads to the question: why are you not earning enough money? The answer is never about the money! Hopefully, you are starting to see what we mean by this.

So, if we live in a world of **cause and effect**, what is causing the results in our lives?

Maybe you are getting that, Aha! feeling – it is our ACTIONS!

What causes our actions? If I am a habitual shopper, what causes this? Our actions are not the real reason, however. Consider the following:

1.   Our actions are the **combined impact of our behaviour,** which is rooted in our beliefs or mindsets – this is both implicit (our subconscious mind) and explicit (our conscious mind).

2.   After that comes our **thoughts,** of which we have about 70, 000 per day. Our thoughts are **filtered through** our Reticular Activation System (RAS) processor, which leads us to our thinking. In this process we form habits that can be constructive and positive, moving us closer to our goals, or destructive and damaging, moving us further away from our goals. Remember when you bought your first Red Golf and suddenly you only saw Red Golf's on the road? That's your RAS hard at work.

3.   Lastly, we are **left with emotions.** These can be pleasant, feel-good emotions, i.e., our brain likes to try new and exciting things or face unpleasant or negative emotions that cause a chain reaction. We would far instead stop taking action if it could prevent us

from having to face fear. This will lead us to lose our motivation to take action in anything that we perceive as negative.

Considering the above information, our relationship with money and our finances, is **more complex** than just what we earn and how we spend it.

Carve your path to becoming a millionaire

On the road to becoming wealthy, people typically begin to think about what they have always wanted to do and what they will leave behind when they are gone. How will they be remembered?

Until you know your **goals and priorities,** it is impossible to create an effective financial freedom plan. You can't plan until you know what you want to do. There's generally no point in setting out on a trip and consulting a map if you **don't have any destination** in mind. You need to know where you are going. An effective financial plan must be tailored to your specific needs and goals.

Every individual's definition of financial freedom is different, but the common goal should be to reach financial security. Since many retirees today are in excellent health and can easily anticipate three decades in retirement, they need to **plan for many years** to come. Financial security will allow you to spend the hours that used to be consumed by work and career on hobbies or activities with friends, old and new.

Many retirees have been able to save a good amount of money during their peak earning years, which they will need to fund **the lifestyle** that they have dreamed about. They may have been advised that they could probably live on a lot less during retirement.

This was incorrect advice. An active life of travel, friends, and fun is expensive.

" *A fool and his money get a lot of publicity.* **"**

— **Al Bernstein**

Identify your goals and dreams.

To start taking control of your inner money game, you need to follow a **process of goal setting.** To bring greater clarity to the course of your financial freedom, you need to take stock of your life goals and organise them by priority.

Just what are your dreams and goals? Write them down as a tangible part of your financial plan. Ask yourself specific questions and write down what comes to mind.

1.   What and who are important to you?
2.   Who do you wish to help? What do you want to learn?
3.   Where do you want to go?
4.   What makes you feel happy? Fulfilled?
5.   What have you always wished you had time to do?
6.   Do you have a 'bucket list'?
7.   Take a peek into your future as you imagine it will be:
    • Do you see yourself traveling?
    • Daily rounds of golf?
    • Indulging in a hobby?
    • Spending time with grandchildren?
    • Do you plan to work part-time or perhaps volunteer for charities?
    • Do you intend to help other family members financially?

If you don't have goals, it is impossible to plan a path. It will definitely be impossible to get clarity on what your future financial position should look like. You will become a rudderless ship on a vast ocean.

Set realistic goals

In your situation **you need to identify** what your **discretionary** and **non-discretionary** expenses are. How much do you want to spend to attain your personal goals, and how much must you spend to survive? Many parents encourage their children to leave South Africa for a more secure future without thinking of how they will afford to travel overseas for visits. Later in the book, we discuss how your non-discretionary expenses should be funded through guaranteed income sources. This means you need never worry about running out of money for your essentials.

It's essential to get a handle on the withdrawal rate **you will need to fund your desired lifestyle.** Consider what will happen if your investments don't go the way you expect. Your lifestyle could change dramatically. You might find yourself unable to keep pace with your golf buddies. If maintaining those relationships is of high importance to you, does your retirement plan allow you to support them under any circumstances? In other words, are you being completely realistic about the kind of lifestyle that your portfolio can provide?

Many people are simply **not clear** about how much they can or cannot take from their portfolio. They don't know what they can afford. No one has taught them this information, so they base their decisions on their experiences. But those experiences can be misleading. For decades, the stock market seemed to head ever upward, as did real estate. Pre-1994, the JSE had an average growth above twenty percent. No wonder endowment growth was projected so high. After exchange controls weakened, however, so did our stock market performance. Thus the 'norm' has changed. Those investors have since faced significant struggles. It's essential to recognise what can happen if you base your lifestyle on the support of fluctuating economic cycles. Like friends, they can let you down.

People in their fifties tend to base their perception of their market's performance on how it fared when they **began their** investment life – in other words, phenomenally. It's only recently, since the turn of the millennium, that their eyes have been opened. It's human nature to turn our experiences into expectations. Retirees, therefore, are led to withdraw from their accounts even as they sink, fully expecting that the market will restore them. After all, that's what happened in the past. But this is not necessarily how the market will perform in the future. Once retirees start those withdrawals, the situation worsens dramatically.

Meanwhile inflation has a disproportionate effect on retirees, as the rapidly rising cost of medical care illustrates. If **high inflation** rears when you are retiring, you can be left devastated. Inflation may have averaged only a few percent a year over the generations, but you're not dealing with an average. You're dealing with you. You're dealing with what you are facing now in the real world, which is why you need to be realistic about your dreams. You have to plan for the worst, even as you are hoping for the best.

Match dreams to resources

It helps to identify the **date** by which you wish to achieve financial independence. You also need to determine what might get in the way of that independence, such as a market correction, significant inflation, an increase in taxes, or health issues. **Your dreams, in other words, must match your resources.** If you don't have a handle on this, you will face troubles, including a feeling of social isolation when your friends leave you behind.

It's been said before that **"People with goals succeed because they have a plan – it is as simple as that."** Quick question: "Do you have a plan?"

Goal setting is that critical process where you determine what your ideal future would look like. Unless you have arrived at utopia, your future world will look different than your current reality. Our greatest challenge to overcome is that our present and future are at odds with each other. Especially when it comes to our financial goals and physical wellbeing. Imagine a world where you can live life as if there were no tomorrow...

Goal setting involves **visualisation** – a process where you "see" your future self, what you do, who you do it with, and how you will be able to afford your future lifestyle. As much as it is still clouded in mystery, the act of visualisation has been proven to work exceptionally well in "creating" that future world. Numerous studies have shown that people who wrote down their goals and visualised them, were significantly more likely to achieve them.

A fantastic exercise you can do to determine your exact dreams and goals is an exercise we call **"Back to the Future"**. If you were born in the '60s or '70s, you would remember a movie by that exact name, where a teenage Michael J Fox time-traveled to a future date, which by the way, was set for 2015!

Start to **visualise the future** you want and apply the skill to write them down. This will help you travel to your future and start building your new reality every day.

Napoleon Hill wrote a fantastic book in the 1920's, that still has some relevance today, titled *"Think and Grow Rich"* which helps with the process of visualisation and mapping your goals in six simple steps:

1. Fix in your mind the **exact detail** of what goals you desire.
2. Determine precisely what you **will give** to achieve your desired goals.
3. Establish the **exact dates** when you want to achieve your goals.
4. Create a **definite plan** to carry out your desired goals.
5. **Write out** all your goals clearly and concisely.
6. **Read** your written statement of goals and desires twice a day, once in the morning and once at night.

In all our research on the most successful individuals, we have observed their ability to set goals and work on them daily in the above way. Successful people have **successful habits** that they follow daily, and it is as simple as that.

A natural practical way to do the above is to sneak a peek into your future and visualise a **perfect day**, 10 or 20 years from today. This day reflects your ideal life where you have achieved all the goals you have set yourself, and you share with the people you care about the most.

Here are the typical questions you have to ask yourself to construct that perfect day!

1. What time do you wake up? Do you set yourself a schedule to achieve something first thing in the morning, such as time for your "Hour of Power"?
2. With whom do you wake up beside you? In your relationship goals, you would have specified who the people in your life would be! This is one of the most important goals to get right!
3. Where do you wake up? In other words, where do you stay

if one of your earlier goals were a specific house or area you would want to stay?

4. What do you do first thing in the morning? In question one, you would have a scheduled time to wake up so that you can do some meditation and praying, maybe a planned morning training session (if so, what would that entail, i.e., would you go to the gym, just go for a run or a cycle session? Also do you train by yourself or with someone specific?).

5. What kind of breakfast do you eat that would be fuel for your body and day? And who do you eat breakfast with?

6. Considering the above two questions, another question would be, "What do you look like?" In other words, in what physical shape are you? The answer to this question undoubtedly lies in how you handle yourself during the day regarding physical wellness, eating, and general wellbeing goals that you live daily by!

7. Do you set out some time for personal development and learning opportunities? What is this, and what does it entail?

8. Once your early morning routines have been done, the next question would be: "What work do you do? Do you drive to my office? Do you work for a specific company? and What do you do? Remember, this is your perfect day! You construct it with your dream career or business.

9. With whom do you share your day? Who are your colleagues in business? Who works with you?

10. Who are the ideal clients you deal with who value your business and professional input? Where do you see them? Do they visit your office or do you call them? What do you discuss? and How do they perceive you?

11. How many hours do you work per day and week?

12. What time do you generally finish work, and what do you do then?

13. Do you have specific ideas for your ideal evening with your loved ones?
14. What do you do at night that will make your day that extra special?
15. What time do you go to bed? Do you do some planning for the next day? Read a book, listen to relaxing music?
16. If your perfect day is a holiday, the question would be, "Where is my ideal holiday destination, what do I do, and who traveled with me?

The questions are mere guidelines for you to work with. Once you have honestly answered all your questions and have an idea of what your perfect day would look like, the question would be: What components of this day can I start executing **right now?** What would this cost me? And how would I start?

CHAPTER FOUR:

HOW DO YOU LIKE TO THINK?

Brains and Brain Profiles

Although brain science has gained impetus and popularity in recent times, the brain has always received its share of fame and notoriety. Aristotle didn't think much of this organ, considered it secondary and thought it was a cooling agent for the heart.

Different opinions on the brain reigned over the centuries. Leonardo Da Vinci hoped his studies of the brain would bring him closer to locate the seat of the soul. Hippocrates (in the 4th century BC) believed the brain to be the seat of intelligence and bizarrely the Greek anatomist Galen theorised that the brain functioned by movement of animal spirits through the ventricles!

One of the most famous brains is of course that of Albert Einstein. An autopsy performed on his brain showed it has an unusually complex pattern of convolutions in the prefrontal cortex, the area that is important for abstract thought.

Harvard maintains a Brain Bank where over 7,000 human brains are stored for research purposes! They certainly think that there is a lot more to find out and learn about our brain.

Luckily with ongoing research, we do know quite a bit about the brain. One aspect of the design of the brain that has intrigued anatomy researchers over the years, is the distinct division of the brain into two halves (referred to as hemispheres). As far back as 400 BC, Hippocrates remarked that 'the brain of man is double' when suspecting that the two halves were not equal. In 1864 Broca, a French surgeon, proved that our verbal center is located in the left side of the brain. The real breakthrough came nearly a century later when a group of doctors performed the first split-brain operation on a few epileptic patients. The research that followed these operations, for the first time revealed the secrets of the two brain hemispheres. It became clear that the two halves controlled vastly different aspects of thought and action. Researchers found that the left brain (which controls the right side of the body) is dominant for language and speech and for analytical and logical thought, while the right brain (controlling the left side of the body) excels at visualising, holistic and unstructured tasks.

An interesting question remained – do people have brain preferences? In other words, do we favour either the left or the right brain in our thinking and doing? This sparked years of research by several people – research that proved two things: all people have brain preferences, but these preferences don't necessarily fall in either the left or the right brain. In other words, it appeared that brain preferences involved the whole brain and its four quadrants. By combining years of research and modern technology, Dr. Kobus Neethling has developed a number of assessment tools (NBI®) that can profile the individual's brain preferences. Over the last 20 years, these brain profiles have been applied in:

- teaching, training and learning
- leadership, management
- many aspects of business
- relationships
- communication
- parenting
- strategising, visions
- values
- sport
- losing weight
- everyday life
- well, just about everything

So, what do brain profiles reveal? They reveal why we differ in the way we prefer to study, to discipline our children, act in close relationships, or to communicate. They reveal why some of us are tidy and others chaotic, why some become accountants and others, artists. And they reveal HOW WE DEAL WITH OUR MONEY!

Some truths about your brain profile

Questions and answers

Understanding your brain profile will unlock a host of insights into your own behavior and the actions of others. But before we discuss your brain profile and the link between brain preferences and wealth, here are the answers to some frequently asked questions:

➤ **Are there good or bad brain profiles?**

Brain profiles show our brain preferences, and cannot be

good or bad, right or wrong. Even when you show a lack of preference for a certain quadrant of the brain, you don't necessarily have a limited competence for those processes – you may have learnt the skills to compensate. We should strive towards understanding, tolerating and valuing those who have different preferences from ours.

➤ **Can brain preferences change?**

They are usually rather fixed, but can change under special circumstances and over a period of time. We can develop our skills even in quadrants where we have low preferences, but it is not often that our thinking preferences change dramatically. You like what you like!!

➤ **What is the best profile?**

There is no best profile. The ideal way of thinking though, is WHOLE BRAIN THINKING. That means you develop the skills to operate in all four quadrants (and 8 dimensions) of the brain in order to be a better parent, manager, teacher, spouse….. and MONEY MANAGER!

The four quadrants and 8 dimensions of the brain

In the following example of a brain profile, you will notice that the left brain is divided into the L1 (top left) and the L2 (bottom left) quadrants and the right brain is divided into the R1 (top right) and the R2 (bottom right) quadrants.

The quadrant scores fall in different categories: 95+ = very high; 80-94 = high; 72-79 = high average; 65-71 = average; 50-64 = low; -50 = very low.

Peter's Brain Profile

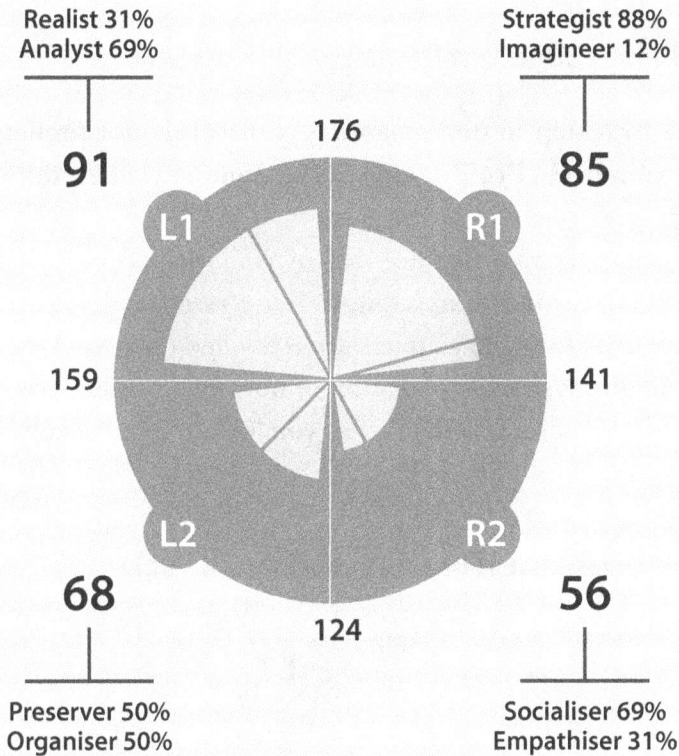

Realist 31%
Analyst 69%

Strategist 88%
Imagineer 12%

176

91

85

L1

R1

159

141

L2

R2

68

56

124

Preserver 50%
Organiser 50%

Socialiser 69%
Empathiser 31%

In this example, Peter has very strong preferences for the processes of the L1 quadrant (91), strong preferences for the R1 quadrant (85), average preferences for the L2 quadrant (68) and low preferences for the R2 quadrant (56).

This will determine the type of parent Peter is, how he manages his employees at work, how his partner experiences him and how he manages his finances.

More about Peter and his 8dimensions brain later...

Interpreting your brain profile

But first ...

Determining your Brain Profile.

The first step in understanding yourself is to complete your NBI® Wealth Brain Profile. This can be done by visiting the website *solutionsfinding.com.*

In order to give you an idea of your preferences, here is a short summary of the thinking and doing associated with the four quadrants of the brain. Each quadrant is divided into two dimensions, and we will give a short explanation of how these differ.

As with Peter's profile above, you will most probably have a combination of these dimensions.

The L1-quadrant (Realist and Analyst)

If you have strong preferences for the L1 quadrant, you will approach situations in a logical, realistic, factual and analytical way.

If you are more of a **Realist** you will want immediate, decisive decisions, but if you are more of an **Analyst,** you like to dig deeper and to get to the bottom of things.

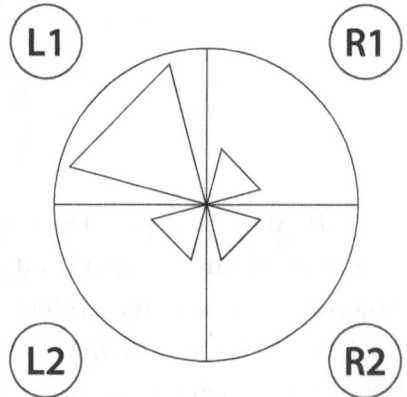

The L2-quadrant (Organiser and Preserver)

If your strong preferences reside in the L2 quadrant you will approach situations in a step by step way, you will do tasks thoroughly, orderly and on time. You will also plan well beforehand.

If you are more of an **Organiser,** you like planning and action, but if you are more of a **Preserver,** you like well-proven methods, loyalty and the status quo.

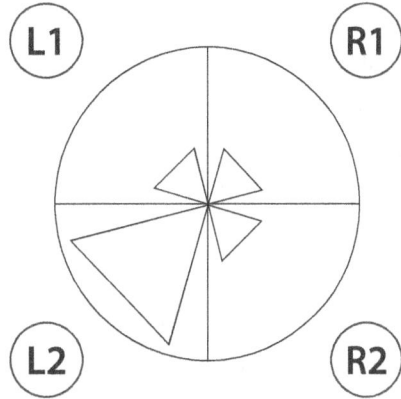

The R1-quadrant (Strategist and Imagineer)

With strong preferences in the R1 quadrant, you are imaginative, curious and like to explore new possibilities. You may be comfortable with a measure of chaos and you keep your eye on the future.

If you are more of a **Strategist,** you take risks in order to create a new future, but if you are more of an **Imagineer,** you like to generate ideas and to be flexible.

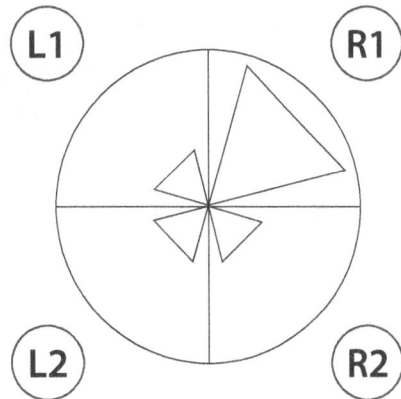

The R2 quadrant (Empathiser and Socialiser)

R2 dominant people are sensitive, would like others to be involved in projects and like interaction. They are supportive, intuitive and usually enthusiastic.

If you are more of an **Empathiser** you like to assist and encourage others, but if you are more of a **Socialiser**, you like team interaction and networking.

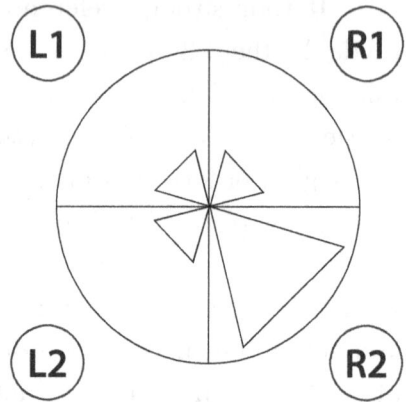

Challenge!

Study your NBI Brain Profile. Keeping in mind that you will not have all the preferences of a quadrant, write a few sentences to describe your approach to finances.

CHAPTER FIVE:

YOUR BRAIN IN ACTION

As we mentioned before, the way you parent your children, train your dogs, (yes really!) manage your relationships and just about any other action or behaviour, depends on your brain preferences.

Before we get into how you manage your money, let us put brain preferences and how they manifest in your life, in perspective.

What is your parenting style?

If this is your profile (strong preferences in the two right brain quadrants and low in the left-brain quadrants), you will most probably not be a very strict parent. You will be loving, affectionate, you will like conversations with your children, you will know their friends and welcome them to your home (R2). You would encourage them to try out new things, not be too strict regarding neatness and other rules, think of interesting places to visit and do things on the spur of the moment with them (R1).

When it comes to careers, you will be open-minded to consider unconventional careers and their happiness will be more important to you than just 'doing well'.

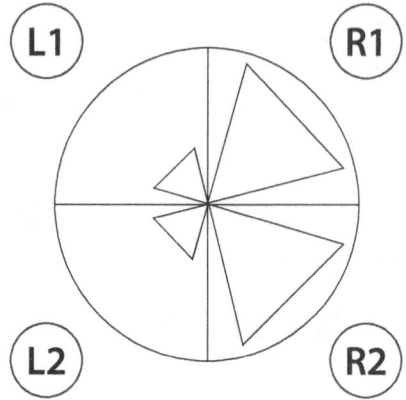

What is your teaching/lecturing/presentation style?

If this is your profile, you are strong in the L2 quadrant and the other quadrants are all low or average. What would this indicate about how you train others? Even if you are not in this kind of job, try to answer these questions before we give it away:

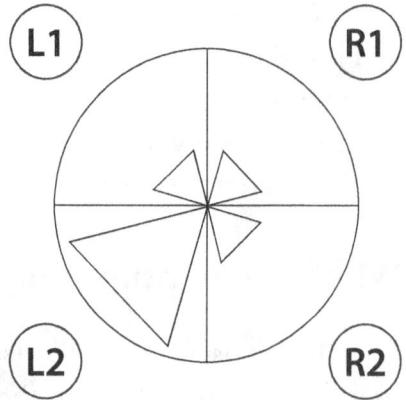

- Would you be disciplined and enforce rules?
- How would you organise your class/presentation room?
- Would you be well prepared?
- How could right brain learners/listeners experience you?
- What would your attitude be towards a fixed syllabus?

Let's see how you did.

You would certainly be very disciplined and expect the participants to follow the rules. Your training room would be very organised, material, handouts ready and prepared. You would not necessarily try to make it homely or 'pretty'! You would always be very well prepared and stick to the syllabus (what else is it there for!!). Right brain participants may experience you as boring at times, because everything always goes according to (the same) plan and there are no surprises.

What kind of a driver are you?

Yes, even the way you drive your vehicle, depends on your brain preferences. There are two major elements of this profile that will have a strong impact on your style of driving, and that is rule bound (L2) and people-focused (R2).

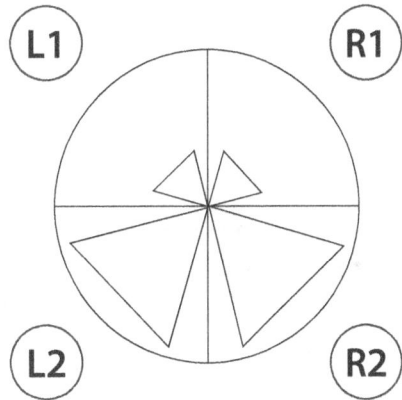

L1   R1
L2   R2

If this is you, you will mostly follow the rules of the road, because of your L2 but also because you are considerate and respectful towards other drivers (R2) and would like to avoid conflict. You would put safety first (L2) and also because you care for your passengers and fellow road-users (R2). On the down-side, you may sometimes be tempted to use your cell phone and be distracted by your passengers because you like being involved in conversations (R2).

Love and your brain!

I don't think we have to tell you that relationships can be tricky! Your brain preferences have a great impact on how you experience your partner and the reasons for conflict or harmony.

So, let's talk about this couple. Here you have Julie who has strong preferences in the quadrants L2 and R2, while John's preferences reside in the L1 and R1. A recipe for disaster?

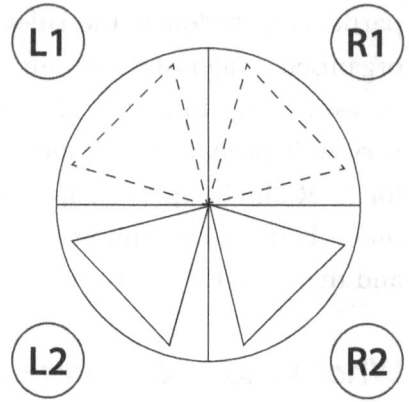

Not necessarily! That is the beauty of understanding how your brain preferences impact your life and then improve it. So, what do we see in this relationship?

- Julie is an organiser and does it with gusto! John on the other hand is very irritated be having his life organised for him. He likes to do his own thing (L1) and does not think organisation is always necessary (R1).
- Julie becomes unhappy because after all she does so much for John, and he seems rather nonchalant about all her efforts.
- Julie longs for security and conflict is therefore not something she handles well.
- She is also traditional and loves traditional ways of celebrating etc. John though, is always looking for variety and excitement.
- The fact that she is always pushing for working through their issues step by step, bores John no end!

- She feels so irritated that he seems to think things will work themselves out!
- Julie is careful, John says let's go!
- She can be romantic (R2), but he is often too busy with all kinds of things, to remember the romantic side of things.

If we understand these differences, we also understand that because our partner is different, does not make him/her wrong.

How do you approach health programs?

Our failure with eating and exercise programs, often comes from the fact that we approach these only from our strong quadrants of the brain, instead of applying the whole brain for success – like in all other situations.

If this is your brain profile, you are on a diet every Monday morning – until Tuesday afternoon! Yes, R1 dominant people tend to lose interest, become bored, find excuses for why they don't need this after all. As a strong R1, you take short cuts, stop weighing and measuring and remove the picture of your future self from the refrigerator!

After these examples, we are sure you get the idea of how important the insight into your brain preferences is in all areas of your life.

Now the BIG QUESTION – WHAT DO THEY HAVE TO DO WITH MY FINANCES?

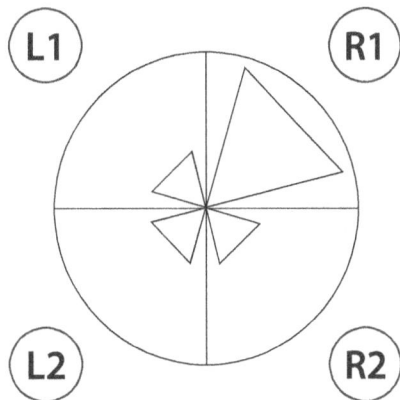

Challenge!

Try to profile some of the people you are close to. Family, colleagues and friends. What does your new insight reveal about each of them and some of their behaviours?

CHAPTER SIX:

YOUR BRAIN AND WEALTH

We hope that by this time you have been convinced that your brain preferences have an impact on all areas of your life. If you do not know how to apply this knowledge, the chances will be good that you will have unhappy and discontented students in your class; that your partner will sometimes feel like screaming because you just don't understand! You will understand that this is the reason you have been unable to stick to diets in the past, and why you may be a very unpopular driver.

Now the essence question of this book – will your insight into your 'money preferences', help you to become rich or manage your money better?

Your financial brain

Important: if you have not completed your NBI brain profile, this would be a good time to do so.

On the other hand, if you think you have a good idea who you are after studying the information on the different brain quadrants, let's get digging into your financial brain!

How do your preferences translate into WEALTH PREFERENCES?

When it comes to interpreting your brain profile with your wealth in mind, the following are important indications:

- How you deal with money
- Why money is important to you
- What kind of financial advisor you prefer
- What the skills are that you lack in order to be financially successful.

REMEMBER, you may have a combination of the dimensions described below. Your brain profile may show 50% in both dimensions, or a close call like 40/60% which indicates that you have preferences in both dimensions.

The L1 and wealth

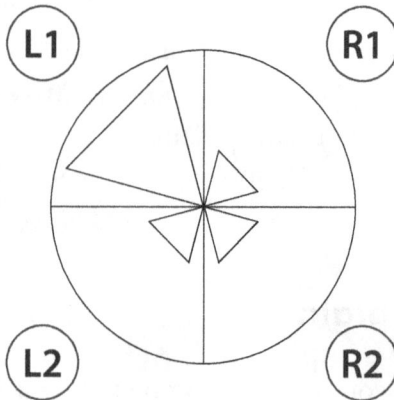

L1 Realist

Rich Brain	Poor Brain
• Money is important to you and you think seriously about it. • You want to see money grow and set clear targets and goals. • Because you are mostly realistic, you will be decisive when money decisions have to be made – you know exactly what you want. • Performance is important to you and you will therefore drive for success, for the best possible outcome and return.	• You want to see results immediately. You therefore become impatient and irritable when things do not move along as expected. • You may also be quite status conscious and this would sometimes encourage you to over spend in order to "compete with the Jones'". • This is made worse because of your competitive nature. • You tend not to ask for or listen to advice and think you know enough to go it alone.

L1 Analyst

Rich Brain	Poor Brain
• You like to research possibilities and make sure of facts before you invest or spend. • You weigh up the pros and cons of any transaction before making a decision. • You want to see your money grow and are constantly making calculations to see how things are going. • Your money decisions are based on clinical facts and research and not on emotions.	• Your 'wanting to get to the bottom of this', may delay important financial decisions. • You can be over critical when it comes to results, investments, people involved in the process. • You tend to be a know-it-all and resist listening to advice. • You are constantly comparing different financial possibilities, weighing up the pros and cons- but not actually going over into action.

L1- Poor brain language: "Do you think I'm Harry Oppenheimer?"

The L2 and wealth

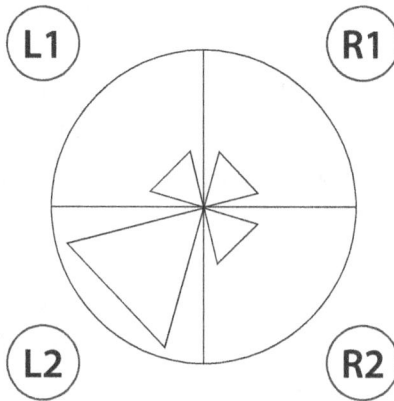

L2 Preserver

Rich Brain	Poor Brain
• You are generally very cautious when it comes to money. • You look for guarantees, testimonials and assurances before any monetary transaction. • You do not spend or invest impulsively and would consider the situation very carefully. • You ensure that you get advice from people who have years of experience.	• You are often too conservative and shy away from anything that may not look absolutely safe. • You are skittish about taking any risk even if it is calculated. • You will only go for an opportunity that is well tried and tested, if proven to have worked in the past and ticks all the safe boxes. • You resist all new and current ways to make money.

L2 Organiser

Rich Brain	Poor Brain
• You tend to keep to your set budget and plan for unforeseen expenses. • Because you are a planner, you keep your retirement, your children's education etc. in mind when you consider your finances. • You know what is going on regarding your finances at all times. • You read contracts, small print, reports very carefully.	• You find it difficult to delegate – you tend to micro-manage anybody involved in your money matters. • Any timeline not met, makes you lose faith in the system or person. • Because you insist on a step-by-step approach, you are easily thrown by new ways of going about making money. • You resist any quick action to get into a good investment – you need to prepare yourself first.

L2- Poor brain language: "Money doesn't grow on trees!"

The R2 and wealth

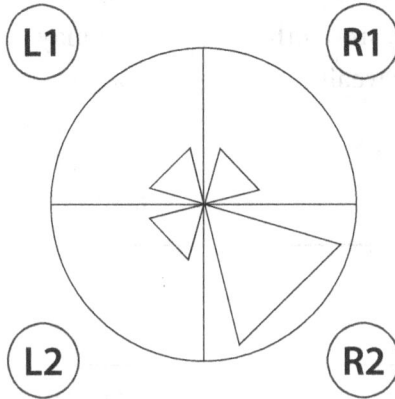

R2 Empathiser

Rich Brain	Poor Brain
• You are passionate about your family and are therefore keen to put money aside for their future. • Because you are intuitive and you have a good insight into people and their motives, you often feel when advice is good or bad. • You build strong relationships with those you trust, and are therefore in a good position to get the right information from the	• You sometimes spend too much on others (gifts for special occasions, treats to make others feel better, on your favourite causes, etc.). • Emotions, moods, the day of the week, etc. can limit your vision and influence your willingness to make financial decisions. • You may be a 'people-pleaser' and therefore do what others close to you expect of you instead of

right people. • Values are important to you and form the basis of ethical growth of your wealth.	going for a great financial opportunity. • You may intuitively know you are getting bad financial advice, but feel too bad to hurt somebody's feelings and go right ahead.

R2 Socialiser

Rich Brain	Poor Brain
• Because special occasions are important to you, you want to save in order to afford celebrations and big events in the future. • You are open to listening to advice – especially if a good relationship has developed between you and your financial advisor. • You become enthusiastic about good investments and ways to make money and will put a lot of energy into the project. • You like to network and so doing gather information	• You often allow your emotions and mood to dictate your financial decisions. • You are seldom decisive and can't make a decision without getting input from several people – and miss the opportunity. • You may also tend to spend too much on yourself because you feel down, you feel you deserve it because of certain situations in your life (therapy sessions, personal rewards, "retail therapy", going out with friends).

regarding financial opportunities and opinions.	• You like to be part of the group, so are swept along in spending sprees, dodgy investments and running up debt to ensure you keep up with the rest.

R2- Poor brain language: "Money is the root of all evil"

The R1 and wealth

R1 Strategist

Rich Brain	Poor Brain
• You see the bigger picture and understand the important role that money plays in just about all aspects of life. • You are prepared to take some risks to make more money. • Because you always have your eye on the future, you are excited about saving money and investing for something you envisage will improve your future. • You are able to see trends and make some of your own predictions and are often ahead of the financial curve.	• Because you loathe plans and long processes, you see the step by step approach that some financial decisions entail, long-winded, unnecessary and unacceptable. • Your decisions can be too risky. • You are impatient, like the excitement of the 'chase' and therefore opt out of investments too soon in order to go after the next thing that excites you. • You like to change the status quo and find unchartered territory – often without proper preparation and safeguards for your money.

R1 Imagineer

Rich Brain	Poor Brain
• You have a strong gut-feel that points to good investments. • You are willing to take risks to make more money. • Because you can visualise your dreams, you very often see the success of financial decisions before they occur. • You are willing to change previous decisions quickly if they seem to be having bad results. • You are often courageous enough to be the first responder if new opportunities are revealed and are in on the initial big gains.	• You are often an impulsive spender. • You dream big, but not always logically!! Your ideas about the future may be rather off the wall and you could spend money on it without the proper research. • Like with most other things, boredom sets in very quickly and you are therefore constantly looking for the next best thing, other ways of making money or to invest, and for the next get-rich-quick scheme. • You like to be unconventional, controversial, bucking the trend – often to your detriment as you do not take the time to do your homework or enough research into the scheme or opportunity.

R1- Poor brain language: "You only live once!" "It's the luck of the draw"

Peter's wealth brain

Let's get back to Peter – we introduced him earlier in the book. We explained his brain profile and general preferences, but let's get to his wealth brain now. Also, let us remind you of his scores: Peter has strong preferences for the processes of the L1 quadrant (91), strong preferences for the R1 quadrant (85), average preferences for the L2 quadrant (68) and low preferences for the R2 quadrant (56).

What we haven't looked at, is Peter's 8 dimension scores and how these will impact his attitude towards money and wealth.

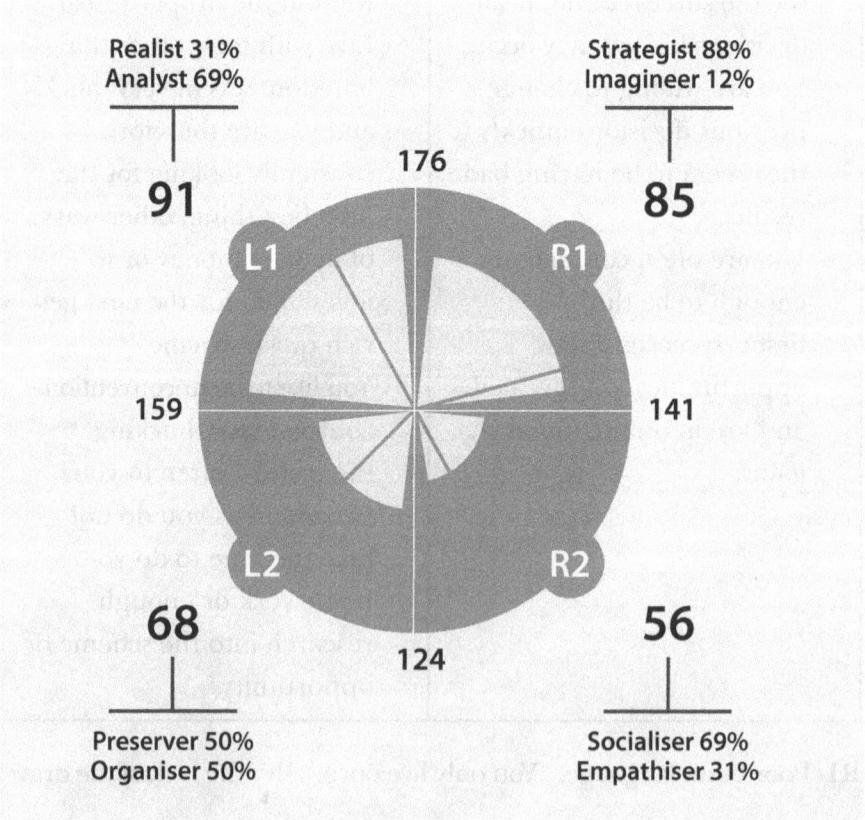

Realist 31%
Analyst 69%

Strategist 88%
Imagineer 12%

91

85

176

L1

R1

159

141

68

56

L2

R2

124

Preserver 50%
Organiser 50%

Socialiser 69%
Empathiser 31%

Looking at his profile, we can conclude that he has a unique relationship with money that will influence his financial decisions in very specific ways. You will recognise some of these descriptions from the explanations of the rich and poor brains of each quadrant.

- In general, money is important to Peter (L1 – strong).
- He certainly would like his money to work for him – now and in the future (L1 Realist – goal-driven, R1 Strategist - future-oriented).
- Although he can be quite critical about any advice he may be given (L1 Analyst), he will listen if it is backed by good and proven research. Also, if the advisor seems to know what he is talking about, talks with authority and can back his advice with facts and figures, he will tend to listen (L1 Analyst – strong).
- As soon as he is expected to fill in endless forms, he will be rather irritated (L2 Organiser – average).
- The same goes for waiting long for results and having to show patience during the process (L2 – average; R1 Strategist – high – excitement dissipates)
- Peter will not be interested in too many "safe" investments and will be more impressed if offered a variety of options (R1 Strategist – high and L2 Preserver – average).
- On the one hand Peter may be status focused (L1) but on the other hand not people-focused (R2 Empathiser – low). Therefore, certain arguments regarding why he should make certain investments and take specific decisions, will not impress him one bit.

The whole-brain and wealth

Hopefully some of your financial decisions of the past are making more sense to you now. What is important though, is to figure out what to do about these insights in the future.

Like with anything else in your life (parenting, training, your sport, managing and communicating), success depends on your ability to make the whole-brain work for you. What does that imply when it comes to wealth? We tend to approach everything we do from our strong preference quadrants and dimensions. If you are a L2 and you want to lose weight for example, you will do some excellent things towards success, like planning beforehand, preparing and sticking to daily eating plans (Organiser). But what can go wrong is that insecurity takes over (the life I'm used to is gone), the drastic changes it asks from you, scuppers you and your inflexibility takes the pleasure out of eating with you for your family and friends (Organiser and Preserver). So, it's best to give up and regain that wonderful security of the life I'm used to.

So, what is the answer to success in all the areas of our lives – also when it comes to wealth? Making the WHOLE-BRAIN work for you. Yes, this is a challenge, because you will sometimes have to learn skills in quadrants and dimensions where you have low preferences. You will have to make sure you move between all the quadrants of the brain in order to achieve financial success.

Your low score quadrants will obviously be your greatest challenge. Going back to dieting, if you are a strong R1, you will have to set specific times aside to plan. You will have to make a concerted effort to stick to the eating plan and use L1 and L2 self-talk to help you through some tough times.

The same principle applies when it comes to how we deal with finances. Here is the whole-brain wealth grid that should become your roadmap for financial success.

Keep this in mind when you complete your wealth plan in Chapter 6.

The whole-brain wealth grid

L1	R1
Realist	*Strategist*
• Make sure you have all the facts at your disposal to make a concerted decision. • Set goals – short and long term.	• Always keep your future in mind. What do you really want as far as wealth is concerned? • You have to be prepared to take some risks.
Analyst	*Imagineer*
• Do research before making any financial decision. • Listen to the professionals.	• Do not disregard your gut-feel about opportunities. • At times, you have to give up something now (immediate gratification in contrast with the long game).

L2	R2
Preserver	*Empathiser*
• Be careful with your money and resist fly by night schemes. • Read contracts etc. thoroughly and double-check (or get somebody trustworthy to do it for you).	• Build a good and trust relationship with your advisor. • Listen to your intuition regarding people and advice.
Organiser	*Socialiser*
• Make sure you know how everything works. • Follow all the steps of the process – do not take short-cuts.	• Be open to listen to a variety of people and opinions. • Be emotionally intelligent regarding money.

Ask the right questions

Use your whole-brain and ask the right questions. Answer all the questions below – they will indicate the direction you should be taking.

WHAT — Realist · Strategist — WHY

Analyst

Imagineer

Preserver

Socialiser

HOW — Organiser · Empathiser — WHO

L1 WHAT?	R1 WHY / WHAT (strategic)?
• What are my short-term/ long-term goals? • What do I really want? • What is the real reason I am not wealthy? • What do I have to stop doing?	• Why do I want to be wealthy? • Why am I not already living the life I want? • What does my future dream look like? • Why do I lose interest/track? • Why multiple income streams?

L2 HOW?	R2 WHO? / HOW? (emotion)
• How do I start? • How do I draw up an effective financial plan? • How do I ensure I take action? • How do I establish successful financial habits? • How do I match my dreams to my resources?	• How do I feel about my finances? • How do I want to feel about my finances? • Who will support me/offer advice? • Who are my negative enablers? • Who do I affect in negative ways if I don't manage my money wisely?

Challenge!

You probably know quite a lot about your attitude towards finances at this stage. At the end of the book, you will be challenged to follow a 29 day diary to get rid of some of your "bad" financial habits. Take the time now to identify some of your POOR BRAIN habits. This will help you to set the goal you want to work towards with the diary.

CHAPTER SEVEN:

YOUR BRAIN AND WEALTH

The final step - Implement your money plan like the rich

Having read the earlier chapters, you are now in a position where you understand WHY you handle money in a certain way and possibly why you could have struggled to manage your money better. Now you just need a PLAN and HOW TO execute your financial plan. It is very much like the workings of a GPS device or app. A GPS has a straightforward function, getting you to your end destination. It works very simply off satellite coordinates that triangulate where you are; if you choose a variation of destination, it will give you options of the quickest route.

Our wealth GPS works in the same manner. We need to understand what the starting point is (Your Personal Budget), what your end destination is (Your Financial Goals, Retirement Plan, or Financial Independence Date), and then lastly, how to tackle the journey (Your Debt Optimisation and Wealth Creation Plan).

Make a commitment

So, how serious are you about this? Are you committed? Or are you somewhat interested in the concept? Would you maybe consider getting out of debt and transforming yourself into wealth? Your intention is critical to your success! Make that decision now! No-one outside of yourself can make that decision and stick with it.

WHERE DID YOU LEARN ABOUT MONEY?

Think about it for a moment; where did you learn about your money management skills?

Our current predicament is not just our fault, sometimes our teachers on our journey to adulthood were most probably not equipped to teach us the fundamentals of managing our finances (mostly because they also didn't know). Most of us did not learn about managing our money from our parents, at school or university. As a skillset we are not educated on the basics of:

1. Planning our finances
2. Budgeting
3. Managing our debt
4. Protecting our risk
5. Managing our Investments and Retirement planning.

These five elements make out the core of your MONEY PLAN. Many professionals are brilliant at their job and profession but have never learned the basics of personal financial management to enable them to execute a simple and workable money plan. One of the biggest atrocities of the 21st century is the fact that financial illiteracy is still one of our biggest challenges and a skillset that is not taught at any school, university or in the workplace.

The good news - You are a millionaire!

South Africans operate in a minimum wage environment. The minimum salary for a full-time domestic is in the region of R2,500 per month. In a forty-year working life, at the minimum wage, they will earn more than R1,200,000. To get an idea of how much you will earn in your lifetime, just multiply your salary, excluding any future increases, by your term and get your number.

Scary stuff if you realise that if you earn R50,000 per month, your earnings will exceed R12,000,000 if you still have twenty years left to work.

The question is then not whether you will earn a million or more, it is how much of this you will keep for yourself and invest wisely for your future.

If you had to keep going down the road you are currently on, what would your financial destination look like? Are you on the road to financial security, independence, abundance or are you on the road that is well-traveled by most people, that ultimately leads to poverty or financial destitution?

1. PLANNING YOUR FINANCES

Planning your finances start with an understanding of the four core elements of your money.

Once you have made a commitment to start your journey, the first step in achieving your financial freedom is to understand the four core elements of your money or the "Financial Planning Matrix".

The four elements comprise the following:

A: Income –

Get a clear understanding of your Income: how much it is and the different elements it is made up of. This is the simplest process for most to understand. As a consideration, your Income is almost never an indicator of your ability to become financially independent.

B: Expenses –

How and on what you spend your money are probably the biggest reasons why you are not able to become financially independent. The very good news is that you have virtually a 100 percent impact to manage the way you spend your money.

C: Surplus –

SURPLUS is the money left after you have subtracted your EXPENSES from your INCOME. Your surplus is thus just a result of the first two elements. To increase your surplus available for savings and investment in growing your asset base, you need to increase your income or decrease your expenses.

D: Assets –

Assets are the vehicles you use to determine whether you will be able to retire financially independent. Initially your ability to leverage your skills or personal resources will generate your income. This income will be used to invest in other assets that will somewhere in future be able to generate additional income.

2. BUDGETING – CREATING THE BLUEPRINT FOR YOUR FINANCIAL FUTURE

Budgeting is a nine letter swear word for most people. It is mostly because they have not been taught the simplest way to do it properly. They simply use the four elements highlighted above.

STEP ONE: Understand your level of INCOME? As a metric, use **R100 as your total income.**

❝ Financial Independence is an event sometime in the future when your assets/investments produce sufficient passive income to exceed your expenses. ❞

As a rich brain individual, you need to understand the above equation more than anything else. THIS is the fundamental difference between financially successful people and those that will never have the ability to retire (97% of the world's population).

Most people's understanding of their income is reserved for one element of the equation, and that is the Salary they earn from a job, or pay themselves if they are self employed. But how much you earn is not as straightforward. Your income is made up of two components:

1.   Active Income – the income most people earn by exchanging their time for the money earned. At some point in time, you would want to replace this income by the second income stream (passive income).

2.   Passive Income – this is produced by the assets you have invested or created over time, that produces an income even if you do not work. The ultimate goal must be to earn all your income passively.

Understanding the difference is critical. Without generating passive income, you will never be able to retire or live a financially free life.

As a rule of thumb, you need to aim for the following ratio (active versus passive):

- 20 – 30 years :   R100 active / R0 passive
- 30 – 40 years :   R 80 active / R20 passive
- 40 – 50 years: R 60 active / R40 passive

- 50 – 60 years: R 40 active / R60 passive
- 60 – 70 years: R 20 active / R80 passive
- 80 plus years: R 0 active / R100 passive

STEP TWO: **What is my current EXPENSES?**

Robert Kiyosaki, brilliant author of *Rich Dad Poor Dad*, said it doesn't really matter how much you earn, what really matters is what you do with your earnings. Most people have no idea how they spend their hard-earned income until it is way too late. Your surplus income today is the best wealth building tool you have for your future.

Your Expenses are made up by two main categories: Needs (or essential expenses) and Wants (discretionary expenses).

Needs/Essential expenses comprise of five main elements (of your R100, R50 should be budgeted for this).

- Home/Rental
- Car/Transport
- Food
- Clothes
- Basic Insurance (Medical Aid, Short Term, Risk Cover)

Wants/Discretionary expenses are made up by the luxuries in life, in other words we can do without it (but it makes life more comfortable). Of your R100, R30 should be budgeted for these.

- Eating out
- Holidays
- Fancy cars
- Expensive gadgets
- Designer clothes...

According to William Feather "a budget tells us what we can't afford, but it doesn't keep us from buying it."

STEP THREE: Understand your SURPLUS (Income less Expenses). This should be at least R20 from the R100 income generated.

You reap what you sow. As much as this is a biblical principle, this is also a life principle. Our future investment and savings are dependent on firstly spending less than what we earn, and then investing the surplus in income generating assets.

The question that will be answered from this exercise is simply: "What is the surplus figure that you are generating every month?" If you don't generate a surplus you will have a zero percent chance to be financially independent in the future. In simpler terms, if you don't sow any seeds, you have a zero percent opportunity to reap a harvest.

If you have an aim to earn R250,000 per month, but you spend R251,000 every month (minus R1,000 per month), you will end destitute. If you earn R50,000 per month and you spend R40,000, generating a surplus of R10,000, and investing this in a sound investment, you are guaranteed to retire financially independent.

The surplus needs to be used to save and invest in the following:
* Emergency Fund
* Savings (short term – less than 12 months)
* Paying of debt
* Investments (long term – longer than 12 months)
* Giving/Tithing

STEP FOUR: INVESTING in Assets (to replace your active income somewhere in the future).

Your surplus generated should be invested in your Assets.

Right now you are your biggest asset. Your ability to generate active income is your biggest asset when you start on your financial independence journey. On the way you need to replace your earning ability with other assets that can generate income (passively). The simplest example is investing in a second property that you rent out. After repaying the debt, you earn R5,000 rent after expenses. To generate R50,000 passive income to replace your salary, you need 10 properties.

Our biggest mistake is to think that our primary residence is an asset. In Robert Kiyosaki's words an asset is a vehicle that generates income, not one that generates expenses. Unless you rent your property on AirBNB, it will cost money, not generate money. Whilst I do qualify my home as an asset, it is a lifestyle asset, and NOT an income generating asset.

1. MANAGING YOUR DEBT

Some anonymous person said: "Running into debt is not so bad. It is running into creditors that hurt." Given that we as South Africans are heavily indebted, most experience the hardship of debt at some point in time. The worst effect of debt however is it's ability to rob you of a financially sound future.

We have been part of many debates on whether to rent or buy a property is better. Depending on your circumstances, your answer could differ from ours. Suppose we have a look at the wealthiest people worldwide. More than half of them owe their riches to a substantial property portfolio. We know of few people who have built significant fortunes and still rent a property!

For most South Africans buying their property would, in most instances, be the biggest purchase they make in their lifetime and they would be considering it their best "investment"! That certainly could be true if you experience great capital appreciation over time. But to utilise the financial benefit you would either have to sell your property, or be able to generate an income from it to be beneficial in later years.

Many experts agree with the notion that an asset is something that generates income, and a liability will cost you money. If you look at your house, most of us will have debt associated with our primary property. Also, we have to pay property taxes, rates, and levies for as long as we live in our houses.

What you should consider is the substantial opportunity that is owning a property would give you. Property is one of the few asset classes you could buy with Other People's Money ("OPM"). This means that you could apply one of the wonders of the world, namely, "leverage" to your accumulation of assets. You must, however, do it on your terms and not the banks', which in all instances only have their bottom line or shareholder's stake at heart. A large part of this chapter is dedicated to helping you get rid of debt sooner rather than later. While debt can be a good thing, allowing you to leverage it, it is only good on your terms, i.e., you cannot repay the debt on the bank's terms. Not only do we want to help you repay debt quicker, but we also want you to use the leverage from this to ramp up building your wealth exponentially.

So, hear us out.

It is unfortunate, but most South Africans will, at some point in their economic active life, accumulate substantial debt, whether it is to finance a car, a house, or other short-term debt such as credit cards or personal loans. The downside, however, is that your debt and the corresponding monthly repayments prohibit you from starting to invest in your wealth platform.

Currently, South Africans spend more than seventy percent of their disposable income on repaying debt. Most people will pay more than R400,000 towards interest in repaying every R500,000 in home loan debt over a 20 or 30 year term.

THE STARTING POINT

As the good witch told Dorothy, when starting her on the Yellow Brick Road to Oz, "It's always best to start at the beginning."

The object of this part of the book is first to help you get out of debt and then use your extra monthly payments to start that journey to building your wealth platform to get to Financial Independence as soon as you can.

Getting rid of debt will give most people the opportunity to start over. It is a chance to rebuild your life to live that elusive dream life, which most people "dream" of and never truly realise. If you look around you, how many of your friends and family can claim that they live their dream?

In most instances, their Money Psychology dictates their happiness, or rather unhappiness. That concept of "money won't buy me happiness" might be accurate. Still, we have not met many "poor" people who are ecstatically happy.

LET'S GIVE YOU AN IDEA OF THE COST OF DEBT

If you buy a home of R1,500,000 and borrow R1,200,000 to finance your home (considering a 20 percent deposit) and repay at a prime lending rate of 9.25 percent, you would pay a total of R2,220,000 over twenty years. For the privilege of borrowing money from a bank, you will have to pay interest of R1,020,000, more than an 85 percent increase on the original capital value.

Here is a question that most people never consider. Considering the figures in the above example, is the interest the total cost on your debt repayment? The answer is, unfortunately, "No!" Consider the following, "Do you pay your home loan with pre- or post-tax money?" You know the answer! "After Tax Money". In this instance, you must work hard enough to earn money, pay tax on it, and then only pay your home loan.

Also, you have what is called an opportunity cost on your money.

If you could invest "Your" MONEY of R1,020,000 in an Investment vehicle at a return rate of 8 percent, you would acquire R2,202,000 over ten years.

This is the actual opportunity cost of your decision to borrow money to pay off debt.

Proverbs 22:7 highlights the biggest reason not to incur debt beyond your means, and that is that "The borrower is a slave to the lender!" If you are indebted right now, ask yourself the simple question: "Has my debt ever felt like freedom? Or is it a measure of my prison sentence?"

We have been conditioned to satisfy our immediate need by using credit cards, overdrafts, personal loans, store accounts and other forms of credit before we qualify for these items we so readily buy on a whim. Consider the following truth: by utilising credit or debt, we exchange our future income (repayments over a period) for immediate satisfaction.

Consider this: buying a TV and financing it over three years, you are exchanging the pleasure of more pixels, a bigger or a curved screen for a portion of your salary for the next 36 months.

Buying a new car over five years, you are exchanging the right to this new vehicle for a chunk of your paycheck over the next sixty months. Buying the latest fancy smartphone, will have you pay it off over the next 24 months, even though it was FREE with the upgrade?

A NEW PATH TO INDEPENDENCE

The American philosopher Earl Nightingale once said, "You are who you are and where you are because of what you have put in your mind."

By changing the way you think about your finances and money management habits, you can start changing your life.

THE "GET RID OF DEBT" PLAN

You need a workable, new plan. The plan is simply called "The Snowball Effect". Start small, like a snowflake. And then another, and another, and before you know it, it will turn into a massive snowball rolling down a steep hill.

Practically this is how it would work in seven simple steps:

- Prioritise your debts (using the formula you'll be given here).
- Make the minimum required monthly payments on all debts except the highest priority debt.
- Add a Snowball Margin to the regular payment on the highest priority debt.
- Continue this payment each month until that debt has been repaid.
- Once paid off, start with the next highest priority debt.
- Now you use the Snowball Margin, PLUS the previous debt's monthly repayment. ADD the two together to the following monthly repayment amount.
- Continue this until the debt has been repaid.
- REPEAT to repay all debt.

The average South African will be able to repay ALL their debt in a period of seven to ten years.

Imagine that! Repaying your debt in the next seven years! Without earning an extra rand worth of additional income!

CALCULATING YOUR PLAN AND TERM

To determine your plan, you need to follow the following simple steps:

STEP 1

Get ALL the information on your outstanding debts together, write down each debts' name

1. total balance
2. and monthly minimum repayment
3. If you have been paying more on your home loan, STOP doing that. Use every extra cent you can spare to your Snowball Margin.

STEP 2

When you have all of this written down, divide the Total Balance (2) amounts by their respective Monthly Payments (3) and write the answer in column 4. For example: Let us say you had a credit card with a R5,000 balance and a minimum monthly payment of R390. You would divide R5,000 by R390 and get an answer of 13. Do not worry about the answer as it doesn't mean anything by itself. It will help you determine the optimal repayment sequence of your debt.

Do this for every debt that you have.

STEP 3

Once you have done this exercise for all debts, you would have determined the priority debt sequence (5). The debt with the lowest answer you mark is the number 1 priority. And so on.

STEP 4

Determine your Snowball Margin. It is any money that you could save with a proper budget. Try to save at least 10 percent of your monthly net income.

Creating your snowball margin

"How in the world do you expect me to save enough money to put a Snowball Margin together?" Watch and learn.

Some basic steps to start putting your elimination plan to work and getting a Snowball margin begins with something as simple as just revisiting your budget and looking for spending that could be postponed or eliminated. The minute you start focusing on getting rid of debt in your life, you will become quite sophisticated in finding ways to stop spending.

Any money that can be labeled non-essential spending, i.e., on luxuries, could fund your Snowball Margin.

Before you bailout, this does not mean you will have to stop all you are spending on any luxury items that you want. It is just a temporary curb on these short-term luxuries that have no long-term positive impact.

Once you have managed to repay all your debt, you will have significant cash flow left to buy these goods cash.

Your aim should be to get an amount equal to 10 percent of your income to use as your Snowball Margin, do not let anything stop you. Any amount will do.

STEP 5

Add your Snowball Margin in Step 4 to your priority debt number 1. Assume your Snowball Margin is R1,000, and your credit card was the priority. You would add R1,000 to the R390 monthly payment, and your NEW Accelerated Monthly Payment amount would be R1,390 (6), repaying your debt in four months (R5,000 divided by R1,390). This becomes the new period in months to pay back debt (7).

STEP 6

Add the total repayment amount to the next highest priority debt. Full monthly payment PLUS Snowball Margin becomes the new accelerated premium.

STEP 7

Continue steps 5 and 6 to determine the total time left to repay debt.

2. PROTECTING OUR RISK: LIKE THE RICH, GET YOURSELF SOME LIFE INSURANCE

Like owning a home, I also cannot stress enough the importance of life and health insurance. No widow or widower has ever said that their spouse died and left them too much life cover. There is too much financial chaos caused by too little provision for life cover, and the struggles that the family must endure are great.

I have often heard people say they "Do not believe in life insurance!" That's brilliant, because it is not a religion of some kind. Life insurance is just the ability to move the risk from you or your spouse dying early from your family to an insurance company.

Remember Old Age. He is there. He is waiting for you, just around the corner. And he is bringing his good buddies Sickness and Death with him.

Everybody will die, whether you care to think about it or not. No one knows when they will perish. The fact is, everybody should purchase some life insurance. As strange as it sounds – appropriate life cover could be one of the best "investments" that can be made to ensure you leave a legacy for your family. The cost of premiums paid versus the pay-out amount is staggering!

This is especially important if you are planning to get married and have children.

The number one problem associated with sudden, accidental death is the cost involved for funeral arrangements and taxes on the deceased's properties and assets. Furthermore, with your passing, your family needs to adjust to the loss of family income.

There is a joke that the loudest funerals are for those people who do not have life insurance. The financial toll imposed on the family left behind is so much that the family members end up crying, not just out of grief, but more from the real struggle of dealing with the expenses that came out of a person's death.

If you share our thinking, you want your family – parents, spouse, and children, to continue enjoying the fruits of your labour, namely the properties, savings, and wealth you have accumulated through your life's work, after you have died.

You do not want them to have difficulty paying for the estate tax of the home and other properties. You will ensure your spouse continues to enjoy living in the house you purchased. Your life insurance policy will help ensure this happens.

If you love your spouse and your children, and you do not want them to suffer tremendously from financial expenses and losses brought about by your death, then please get some life insurance and make them your beneficiaries.

Please note that a life insurance policy is not meant to provide a windfall of cash to the family left behind. Sure, you can use it for that purpose. But it should be used to help the people left behind to get back on their feet, as painlessly and as soon as humanly possible, so they can adjust to life quickly after you are gone.

3. INVESTMENTS AND RETIREMENT - CREATING WEALTH LIKE THE RICH BY LEVERAGING YOUR MONEY

According to Alfred Marshall "Capital is that part of wealth which is devoted to obtaining further wealth."

Have you ever thought what the wealthy, like Warren Buffet, do differently to leverage their money, invest, earn, reinvest, and earn even more?

The answer is simple: they like taking calculated risks. Calculated risks are those that have some probability attached to them. For example, even if you may suffer a loss, there will be a limit to it. Usually, this limit is either pre-decided or anticipated.

Coming back to the question: what does Warren Buffet do differently? The best way to explain Warren and other professionals like him is a lesson learned from Tony Robbins and Mark Ford called "The Three Bucket Investment" approach. The first bucket is your Security Bucket, the second is your Growth Bucket and the third your Dream Bucket.

First Things First - Build Your Emergency Fund Before You Begin Investing

YOUR SECURITY BUCKET COVERS ALL EMERGENCIES.

Emergencies. We have all experienced emergencies at one time or another, most of them involving money or financing of some sort. The path to prosperity and wealth begins with preparing for emergencies. It is not a question of whether it will happen, but when it will happen.

SCENARIO 1

Your mother called. Your father was rushed to the hospital due to stomach pains he experienced. He does not have any medical aid since he's already retired. They need your help in settling the hospital bills and paying for medication.

SCENARIO 2

One Friday afternoon, on the same day you are planning to go out with your friends to celebrate a friend's promotion, your boss calls you into his office. Beside him is the HR Manager. Although you have contributed a lot to the company, your position was made redundant. Ouch! You? Of all people? You are the Mark Zuckerberg and Steve Jobs of what you do! How can they do this to you?!

The cold, hard truth is, layoffs happen all the time. No one is exempt from them. Even if you are the expert or guru in your position, your company can decide one day that they're better off hiring 2-3 good people to do the work you're doing. In all practicality, they do not need an expert. They just need good people.

SCENARIO 3

The alarm clock rang. You hate it. You want to call in sick. Today, Tomorrow, and The Day After. You have lost your passion for your workplace and for what you are doing. You want to get out. You want to do that thing you were born to do, which your conscious and subconscious minds are pushing you to do. But you cannot. You have bills to pay. The bills come like clockwork. They always do.

If you have saved up an emergency fund, you can use it in any of these scenarios. You can use it for anything. It can be that your car needs repairing, you need to fix a leaking roof, etc.

Your emergency fund will keep you from touching your other savings, your investments. So, the question? How big should your emergency fund be?

As a rule, your emergency fund should be big enough to cover all your expenses for three to six months without you earning a single cent. This will depend on your lifestyle and your situation. If you are the sole breadwinner, then it will be a considerable sum. If you are single and only responsible for yourself, then it will be a smaller amount.

No matter what the amount, there is no need to rush. That is right. There is no need to rush. Your emergency fund is not meant to be completed in a short amount of time. So, take your time. Just make it automatic and make it habitual. Just 10 percent of your net income every month will do, or a lot more, if you can manage.

BUILD YOUR SECOND BUCKET FOR GROWTH.

Famous billionaire of the early 1900's, Andrew Carnegie, said "The way to become rich is to put all your eggs in one basket and then watch that basket."

Congratulations on filling your emergency bucket! Well done.

Now, it is time to build your investment portfolio. Wealth is not created overnight; it takes hard work and planning. The owners of Nando's chicken often say that it "took them sixteen years to become an overnight success!"

There are different types of investment vehicles you can choose from:

- Property.
- Life Insurance.
- Unit Trusts.
- Government Bonds.
- The Stock Market.

These are the most common types. Others include putting up a business, investing in gold or jewelry, investing in commodities, etc.

We will focus on the ones mentioned above. All of these will be used to start filling bucket number two. Remember, this is an ongoing process that will only stop when you have reached financial independence and retirement. If you have secured multiple incomes, this will continue until the day you die and beyond, leaving a sure legacy for your beneficiaries.

START INVESTING TODAY

Now that you have completed your emergency fund and have paid off all your bad debts, it is time to begin investing. If you start working at age twenty and retire at the age of sixty-five, this gives you forty-five years to plan and prepare for your retirement.

Not bad. If you live only up to the age of seventy, this means that you will only have five years to worry about and plan for. Sounds good? Absolutely.

But what if you live up to the age of eighty, ninety, or a hundred? It means that your entire retirement years will be fifteen, twenty-five, and thirty-five years, respectively. So, it means that you must plan and prepare for how you will support yourself for fifteen, twenty-five, and thirty-five years after retirement. Suddenly, it sounds daunting. Suddenly, it sounds overwhelmingly impossible.

You must understand that people are living longer and longer as the years go by. You will live longer than your parents. And your children will live longer than you. Sure, you might not even reach the age of retirement because of your hypertension or high blood pressure, which runs in your family.

But what if you do?

Ensure that how you manage your finances today will provide you with the most comfortable living condition you can imagine, or it will be exceedingly difficult for you in your old age. Your old age is when you should not be worrying about paying for your medicines, food, or utility bills.

Your retirement years are the time you should spend with your children and grandchildren and not become a burden to them.

Investing in your retirement is a mindset. It is a way of life. It is not a love for money but respect for money itself. It is setting aside 20-30 percent of your income every month in unit trusts, government bonds, or buying small amounts of equities each month, stocks from blue-chip companies, which will still be there after your grandchildren have their kids.

Investing in your retirement is not a get-rich-quick scheme. It is ensuring that you will retire comfortably in your old age. It is a constant reminder not to consume all your income every month.

It is a commitment, and a promise that you're making to yourself, that you will not rely on that measly government pension and that you will not burden your children and their families in the future, with your cost of living. It is a hope that you will live in the most comfortable way possible, in your old age.

YOUR R5 A DAY WEALTH PLAN

Most people who do not invest in their future, use the simple excuse of "I don't have enough money to start!"

The easiest way to debunk this excuse forever is to start with five rand a day. You might ask, "What good will that do?" Great question, let us show you.

Five rand invested every day is roughly hundred and fifty rand per month. Hundred and fifty rand per month invested at a ten percent rate of return over forty years is in excess of one million rand. Yes, that is correct, every five rand invested will give you a million rand in the future. Fifty rand a day, would equate to in excess of ten million rand in the future.

If you followed the debt repayment example in the section mentioned earlier. Imagine if you repay your debt in the next seven to ten years, and you utilise the full monthly premium you are currently paying towards your investment plan or growth bucket?

This is how the truly "Rich" do it. They start early, with a small amount, and just add the magic of compounding returns over time to their advantage. As Albert Einstein famously said: "Compound interest is the eighth wonder of the world. He who understands it, earns it; he who doesn't, pays it." Start using this power to your advantage. The sooner you begin the more leverage you will have.

THE LAST INVESTMENT BUCKET IS YOUR DREAM BUCKET

Once you start filling your Growth Bucket, the last bucket to fill is your Dream Bucket. This is the one that you use to fulfill any dream you have. Whether it is to go on a cruise ship around the world, a simple holiday, or that fancy sportscar you've always dreamt of.

Every year use a third of the "growth" in your growth bucket to fill your dream bucket. As a simple example. You have a thousand rand invested in your growth bucket and it grows at ten percent. The hundred rand return is then split in one third going in your dream bucket and two thirds being reinvested in your growth bucket.

Doing this will ensure that you can still enjoy live to its fullest by not scaling down your dream goals. Just make sure that you fill them from the right bucket.

CHAPTER EIGHT:

TAKE CONTROL – CHANGE YOUR HABITS!

The Rich Brain Diary

Habits are formed over time and many people become quite accustomed to their way of doing things. There are good habits and bad habits. All habits should, however, be reconsidered regularly so that healthy habits can improve and bad ones can be replaced by positive habits. Remember, your brain doesn't really mind what you put in, but whatever it is, it will definitely have an outcome. If you constantly send negative thoughts to your brain, like "I can't keep up", "I will never have financial stability" then you will eventually turn into a negative person. The opposite is also true. Think positive thoughts, and you will become a positive and inspiring person who can take charge of your finances.

This diary is designed to help you get rid of any bad money habits.

Why would you want to continue with a bad habit that destroys your self-belief, your future dreams and often also your relationships, when it's possible to turn your back on all the bad habits that make you depressed and uncertain?

This 29-day program is not only intended to bring about short-term change, but also to anchor new habits, to establish positive thinking and to maintain it. The Greek philosopher Aristotle said: "We are what we repeatedly do. Excellence, then, is not an act, but a habit."

Decisive factors for the next 29 days

- Focus on ONE habit at a time regarding your financial independence for the next few weeks. You can start the process again with another habit you would like to change.
- Use this diary to record your progress daily. Don't skip a single day!
- As soon as you commit to this program, you're responsible to continue doing so.
- Before you start the program, first identify all the things that you associate with your bad habit. Think about everything that possibly prompts your habit, for example, you spend money impulsively, you always follow your own mind and do not listen to others. Use stickers in your immediate environment to remind you of your new habit, like "I only spend when I actually have the money".
- Avoid negative behaviour at all costs, for example:
  - To blame and criticise others
  - To get stuck in the past
  - Focus on the bad stuff
  - Self-pity
  - Excuses

- Fault-finding
- Sarcasm
- Moaning
- Procrastination
- Gossip
- To shut off your thoughts too early.
- Each activity fits in one or more of the brain quadrants. Some will therefore be more enjoyable than others for you. Remember how important it is to use your whole brain!

HOW TO USE THE DIARY

- The first few days on the program will feel difficult – and it is – but as you persist every day, the stronghold of the old habits will start to fade and it will become easier to follow your new habits.
- On each of the following 29 days, we give you a MANTRA or confirmation. Repeat it continuously throughout the day. In the beginning, these mantras provide a deliberate way of influencing your thoughts and feelings. If you continue with it, it becomes a spontaneous part of the way you think and feel.
- Complete the activity every day. Everyone is able to change bad habits into good ones, but remember, no one can make choices on your behalf – you choose your own thoughts and emotions. You can never blame others for the thoughts that you choose.
- Use the diary to keep record of your emotions and experiences.
- The themes of the 29 days are:
  - Stay Motivated: Day 1 to 7
  - The Attitude Phase: Day 8 to 14
  - Perseverance: Make Sure You Stay on Track: Day 15 to 21
  - Live Your New Goal: Day 22 to 28
  - Celebrate Your Victory: Day 29

YOUR ULTIMATE GOAL

Write in one sentence what you want to achieve at the end of this program.

Some examples are: I want to be financially independent; I want to speak the language of abundance, not lack; I want to apply my whole brain in managing my finances; I want to plan my financial future.

I (name) _____will

_____
Signed

_____
Date

Day 1: Stay Motivated
I'm on my way to success!

Your activity for today: Today is the first day on your journey to reach your goal. Write down all the small steps today that you're going to take today to reach your specific goal. Be specific.

L2 Morning:	R2 Evening:
Which steps am I going to apply today?	My positive thoughts and emotions about my Day 1 experiences.

Day 2: Stay Motivated
I'm excited!

Your activity for today: Look at the reasons (the why) you've decided to follow this specific program again today. Write your reasons down in a positive style, for example:

I want to be more self-confident and feel financially secure.

I have a specific dream I want to achieve.

R1 Morning:	L1 Evening:
My positive Why statements.	Determine the value of each statement as you experience them NOW on a scale of 1–5 (5 = perfect; 1 = extremely low). At this stage, the low scores should be strong motivators to encourage you!

Day 3: Stay Motivated
Nothing is going to stand in my way!

Your activity for today: Which major obstacles are still blocking the way to reaching your goal?

L1, L2 Morning:	L1, L2 Evening:
My biggest obstacles (e.g. I speak the language of lack instead of abundance – e.g. that is too expensive, I can't afford that; I allow my emotions to guide my financial decisions).	How I can overcome/did overcome these obstacles (e.g. I studied some financial terms to add to my 'rich brain' financial language; I analysed the 'why' of my emotions to understand them better).

Day 4: Stay Motivated
I am not alone!

Your activity for today: It is extremely important to have a support system in place when you start such a program. Make a list of people who can support you in one or other way. Write down their names and the type of support that they can offer you (encouragement, advice, professional support, etc.).

Make sure they know that you are depending on them! If you are not R2 strong, this might prove a challenge, but that is why you have embarked on this journey!

L1, L2 Morning:	*L1, L2 Evening:*
People who can support me.	How do/can they support me? (This question and answer should form a permanent part of your program. You can regularly add to the list.)

Day 5: Stay Motivated
I take action!

Your activity for today: Write down the name of the person that you regard as a role model for positive, rich brain thinking. Which characteristics of that person make an impression on you, and how can you imitate such behaviour?

R2, L2 Morning:	R2, L1 Evening:
Who is my role model and what are his or her positive characteristics?	How can I imitate them? Think of whole brain possibilities, e.g. knowledgeable (L1), an excellent planner (L2), caring about others (R2), visionary (R1).

Day 6: Stay Motivated
I can't wait to see results!

Your activity for today: Start spreading the excitement today! Tell others about the Rich Brain program you're following. Share the results and make others excited about it as well!

Whole brain Morning:	*R2 Evening:*
What can I share with others about the rich brain program so far? Think of changes you have made to reach your goal: e.g. language, attitude, money habits.	How did it feel to share my positive experiences with others?

Day 7: Stay Motivated
Success awaits!

Your activity for today: Reflect on the past seven days. What worked out well, and which obstacles do you still need to overcome?

L1, R2 Morning:	L1, L2 Evening:
What worked well this past week? How do you feel about your successes? What did you do differently (your language, the time you spent planning your budget, talking to a professional etc.)?	Which obstacles remain in my way?

Day 8: The Attitude Phase
I radiate self-confidence!

Your activity for today: This week the focus falls on how you turn your thoughts and emotions into actions.

It is an important phase of the 29-day program, because now your positive attitude will begin to show in all earnestness. Write down how you create a rich brain attitude around you.

R2, L2 Morning:	R2, R1 Evening:
How am I going to spread the rich brain attitude today? For example, think of how you can turn your "wealthy thermostat" up by changing repetitive "poor" statements into "rich" statements.	How does it feel to positively influence the lives of others? What future impact could this have?

Day 9: The Attitude Phase
I have a new approach to finances!

Your activity for today: During the first week, you have probably experienced moments of low self-esteem and uncertainty. You've viewed it as setbacks. Write down how you've overcome those moments, and how you have regained your confidence. Also write down how you are going to handle these moments in future.

L2, R2 Morning:	L1, R1 Evening:
Which moments of low self-image or uncertainty regarding my finances did I experience during Week 1?	How did I (or can I) overcome those moments? What can I do differently?

Day 10: The Attitude Phase
I am creating positive habits!

Your activity for today: Although you've written down your goals and smaller steps to reach them, you have probably experienced some moments of doubts. Will you really be able to change these old habits into lasting new behaviours?

How can you better handle those moments in future?

L1, R1 Morning:	L1, R1 Evening:
What are the moments of doubt about my end goal that I have already experienced? For example, too many moments of sliding back; I am not too optimistic about what I can achieve; I've tried to change my money habits before but...	How did I (can I) overcome these moments? Reread the Whole-brain Wealth grid in chapter 5 to find some answers.

Day 11: The Attitude Phase
I see the finish line!

Your activity for today: One of the best ways to stay positive is to constantly be busy with positive self-talk. Make today a HUGE positive self-talk day (while you drive, at your desk, in front of your computer, wherever). Conduct positive self-talk!

L1, R2 Morning:	L1, R2 Evening:
I commit myself to positive self-talk only. Avoid the pitfalls: I can't afford this, it's too expensive, I will never be this lucky, other people have all the success, etc.	I contemplate my experience of self-talk. Can this become part of me every day?

Day 12: The Attitude Phase
I choose what i think!

Your activity for today: Today is COUNT-TO-TEN-day.

Every time you want to become angry, worried or self-conscious, count to ten and choose a positive reaction. We can always choose what we think, and today you're going to prove it!

L1, R, R1, Morning:	L1 Evening:
Think about situations, people or certain times when you're more likely to think and feel negative – now you're ready to fight them (the situations, not the people)!	Reflect on how you've done, and which positive thoughts worked best.

Day 13: The Attitude Phase
I'm making an even bigger effort!

Your activity for today: The more effort you put in, the better you will feel about yourself and your chances of success.

Today you are going to try extra hard to put more energy and effort into the program. Think about ways to improve your results (it will depend on your original goal).

Examples: less impulse buying (goal = I want to get out of debt); I will work on my financial plan (goal = I will stick to my budget); I will avoid certain activities that cause stress (goal = I will stop shopping to make me feel better).

L2, R1 Morning:	R2, L2 Evening:
Write down all the ways you can think of to add more value to the program. Revisit the Whole-brain Question chart in chapter 5.	How did these extras make you feel today? Can you think of more things to add to your program?

Day 14: The Attitude Phase
I will win!

Your activity for today: Today is the last day of Week 2 of the program. Make sure that a positive attitude is part of your approach for the next couple of weeks. Sometimes you have to be reminded of what a positive attitude means. Today you are going to write your own positive mottos and inspiration on stickers and put them up where you work or at home. Repeat them in your mind every time you see them.

L2, R1 Morning:	L1, R2 Evening:
Write down different quotes and sayings on stickers and put them up around the house or at work. Repeat them during the day.	What difference did these sayings make to your attitude today?

Day 15: Perseverance
I can!

Your activity for today: You are halfway there! Maybe you feel a bit discouraged or unhappy with your progress in the days ahead. Choose the face that best describes you at the moment.

To endure to the end, you'll have to change your negative **emotions** into positive emotions. If at this stage you're happy with your progress, celebrate it!

L2, R2 Morning:	L1, R1 Evening:
Write down the specific negative emotions that you experienced (like frustration, anger, discouragement, inferiority, embarrassment). Keep record of your negative reactions throughout the day.	Reflect on all the negative emotions that you experienced today. Rewrite each one, but add a BUT to the statement (e.g., I'm angry, but tomorrow I'll make better choices; I feel inferior, but I know I have inner strength hidden inside me).

Day 16: Perseverance
I'll persevere to the end!

Your activity for today: Oftentimes it is fear that keeps us from succeeding. Even if it's hard and painful sometimes to overcome your fears, confront them head-on. You can perhaps be fearful of destructive criticism, to be embarrassed, self-sabotage (I always mess things up), etc. Don't allow fear to paralyse or hinder you.

L2, R2, L1 Morning:	L1, R1 Evening:
Write down all the fears that you've experienced up to now, and the things that have hindered your progress. Look them straight in the eye; take control of your fears and don't allow them to control you.	Reflect on how you've handled your fears today. Which lessons on fear and courage can you take with you for the next couple of weeks?

Day 17: Perseverance
I will hang in there!

Your activity for today: Perseverance has been described in the past as "keeping your goal in mind". Today you will re-examine your goal once more. On Day 2 you have also written down the reasons why you've decided to follow this specific program. Look at your list with new perspective and write down the BENEFITS that you'll experience when you successfully complete the program.

L1, L2 Morning:	L1, R2 Evening:
After you've studied your goal, write down all the benefits that the program holds for you. For example, ownership of my financial independence, effective financial planning, my dream in sight.	Which of the benefits on your list have you experienced already? How do you feel about it?

Day 18: Perseverance
I am confident!

Your activity for today: Sometimes it can feel like we've hit a brick wall because we try the same thing over and over without success. Today you are going to take a **fresh approach, maybe even do the OPPOSITE.** Think about which approach didn't work for you, and how you can try to implement something new.

L2, R1 Morning:	L1, R2 Evening:
Make a list of everything regarding the program that didn't work for you (e.g. working daily on a spending plan, talking to several people about how to save, keeping quiet when others impede my progress). Try the opposite today (e.g. a monthly budget instead of daily; make an appointment with a financial professional instead of talking to Tom, Dick and Harry; tell people in a calm and collected way why their remarks/actions bother you).	How did your new approach work? Is there anything that you thought of during the day that you could approach differently?

Day 19: Perseverance
I think positive thoughts!

Your activity for today: It is often our **SELF-DEFEATING BELIEFS** (things that we believe guarantee our failure) that hamper our progress. Today you are going to write down these **beliefs** and change them into positive convictions.

Here is a list of such self-defeating beliefs:

- I'm not allowed to make a mistake or fail.
- I only feel worthy when I get others' approval.
- I'm worthless because I make mistakes.
- I have to be perfect to be truly happy.
- Life is not worth it when I'm financially insecure (my money-making ideas fail, etc.).
- There is something wrong with me if I'm not always confident and happy.

L2, R1 Morning:	R2, L1 Evening:
Make a list of all your self-defeating convictions.	Rewrite them as positive statements, for example: Mistakes are opportunities to learn to do something differently next time. Reflect on how you've applied your positive beliefs today, and what the outcome was.

Day 20: Perseverance
I am responsible!

Your activity for today: With perseverance comes **responsibility.** It's easy to blame others for our wrong actions or negative circumstances. Remember, you make your own choices.

Other people can't MAKE you angry, or negative or stressed!

Today you are going to look at the people and things that you blame when things don't go your way.

L2, L1 Morning:	L1, R2 Evening:
Make a list of people, situations or experiences that you tend to blame when things don't go according to plan (e.g. long working hours, not getting paid enough, bad advice of the past etc.). Stop the blaming game, and take responsibility for yourself today!	How did you change your attitude today by accepting responsibility for your actions? How do you feel about it?

Day 21: Perseverance
I am determined!

Your activity for today: The great Albert Einstein said:

"It's not that I'm so smart, it's just that I stay with problems longer."

This says a lot about **perseverance.** You have eight days left of your program. You have many positive qualities that make you a diehard! Make a list of these characteristics and look at them regularly over the next week.

L2 Morning:	L2, R2 Evening:
Make a list of all your positive character traits that make you a person who perseveres until the end. Don't sell yourself short! Which of these character traits are you going to apply today?	Reward yourself because you practically applied your positive qualities!

Day 22: Live Your New Goal
I am a doer!

Your activity for today: It is said that success is achieved through the **willingness to take action.** You have one week left on the program, and now it's really time to take action! We know now that you have already made a huge effort to reach your goals, but we believe a fresh volley of actions are what you need to move closer to realising your goal. Only 5% of people write their goals down, so, you're already far ahead of most people! Even worse, only 1% of people regularly review their goals! You've already looked at your goals again, also at the reasons behind your goal and its benefits. Read through them again today, so that you don't lose sight of where you're heading.

L1, L2, R1 Morning:	L2, R1 Evening:
Read through your goals as well as the benefits and reasons behind your decision. Add benefits to the list which you've discovered in the meanwhile, and why you want to achieve your goal.	Make a list of disadvantages or losses when you don't reach your goal. Use it as motivation to try even harder!

Day 23: Live Your New Goal
I speak positive words!

Your activity for today: If you want to reach a new goal, you will have to use positive language. Pay attention to how you speak and the words you use every day, and avoid the following completely:

- To complain all the time – rather find solutions.
- To find fault with others and their ideas – rather find possibilities in them.
- To blame others – rather accept responsibility.
- To be aggressive and use swearwords – rather choose patience.
- To gossip and belittle others – rather find something positive to say about each person.

L2, R1 Morning:	L2, R1 Evening:
Make a list of all the examples mentioned above (or any other ones that you can think of) that you're guilty of. Make a special effort to replace it with positive alternatives.	Write down how you're going to change your negative talk that persists into positive speech.

Day 24: Live Your New Goal
I taste success!

Your activity for today: Walt Disney said: *"If you can dream it, you can do it!"* By imagining yourself reaching your goal, you're busy creating your reality in a powerful way. This is how many athletes succeed. Today you are going to imagine yourself in this way – as if you have already reached your goal.

R1, R2 Morning:	R1, R2 Evening:
Close your eyes and picture yourself after you've reached your goal. Imagine that perfect day. Visualise how you act, what you feel and experience; get into the detail; also, how others react. Do this exercise a couple of times today.	Repeat this visualisation exercise, but keep the big picture in your mind for longer and more intensely – really express the new you!

Day 25: Live Your New Goal
Nothing can stop me!

Your activity for today: If you want to be a winner, you have to plant a tiny seed in your brain, and constantly give it water and nurture it in order to make it grow. Your goal is that tiny seed.

On Day 2, you wrote down reasons why you are following this program. Write them down here, and add a new value to each one as you're experiencing them now. We believe that you have nourished your goal for the past 24 days in many positive ways, and therefore you will be able to add more value to each point.

L2, L1 Morning:	L2, L1 Evening:
Make a list of all the reasons/ the WHYs you wrote down on Day 2, also the original value that you've attached to it.	Re-evaluate the reasons as you experience them now. Think about the results.

Day 26: Live Your New Goal
It's now or never!

Your activity for today: One of the most difficult things to do when you pursue a goal and want to change a habit, is to give certain things up. Today you are going to face these things head-on – everything you have to give up (or had to give up already) in order to reach your goal. Remember, you don't just need to pursue your goal for 29 days, but from now on constantly live your dream.

Certain habits, routines and lifestyle choices will have to be eliminated completely.

L2, L1, R1 Morning:	L1, R1 Evening:
Make a list of all the things you want to or have to get rid of, give up or change in order to live your goal. Examples: the security of the well-known; living day to day financially depending on others (entitlement).	Rate each point on your list according to a scale of 1–5 (1 = not difficult; 5 = very difficult to give up). See the high scores as a challenge and inspiration and not as a stumbling block!

Day 27: Live Your New Goal
My dreams are coming true!

Your activity for today: We all have core values which determine how we act and the choices we make. If you really want to live your dream and goal, it must be supported by your strong values. Today you are going to make a list of core values and **write down why your goal is important for each of these values.** Included is a list of values, but there are many others to add to the list: family, loyalty, honesty/integrity, money/wealth, responsibility, flexibility, empathy, self-control, diligence, personal growth, respect, passion, humility, discipline, excellence, courage, perseverance, security.

Here are a couple of examples:

- Family: I can't give my best to my family if I'm unhappy with myself and my financial position.
- Honesty: Honesty also includes being honest about how I can improve my behavior regarding money.
- Self-control: If I can't control my habits, I can't claim self-control as one of my strong values.

L2, R2 Morning:	L1, R1 Evening:
Make a list of all your core values.	Write one sentence about each value and why your goal is important to live this value.

Day 28: Live Your New Goal
I'm giving my all!

Your activity for today: You have almost reached the end of your 29-day program. Today you are going to draw a picture depicting the last 28 days. You don't need to be an artist! It is just a fun way to give expression to the important journey you've undertaken.

R1 Morning:	R1, L1 Evening:
Draw a picture (or more than one picture) to portray your 29-day journey.	Study your drawings and indicate the lows and highs of your story. Think of the highs and give your story a name.

Day 29: Celebrate Your Victory
I am a success story!

Your activity for today: Yes, you've made it! It is a day to celebrate! There are many ways to celebrate your success when you've reached a goal: Tell others about it, reward yourself, host a "joy and gratitude party" or make a victory banner! Remember, it's not the end of the road for you, it's just the beginning. The best reward is to live out your goal and new habits from now one. SUCCESS!

R2, R1 Morning:	R2, R1 Evening:
Celebrate! Think of special ways to celebrate your victory today.	Celebrate! Write a letter to yourself where you congratulate yourself.

ADDENDUM

Your worksheets

_____

_____

_____

_____

_____

_____

_____

_____

_____

_____

_____

_____

_____

_____

_____

_____

_____

_____

_____

_____

_____